David. Christmas 1975. love Pamela.

Wine and Beermaking at Home

Wine and Beermaking at Home

Kenneth Hill

WILLIAM LUSCOMBE PUBLISHER LTD
In association with Mitchell Beazley Limited

First published in Great Britain by
William Luscombe Publisher Ltd.,
The Mitchell Beazley Group,
Artists House,
14–15 Manette Street,
London, W1V 5LB.
1974

ISBN 0 86002 031 2

Printed in Great Britain
Filmset in Monophoto Garamond
by Trade Spools, Frome and
printed by Alden & Mowbray Ltd., Oxford

Contents

Illustrations

Part One
Winemaking

Chapter 1
Introduction to Winemaking

Country wines were first made by the country folk and it was mainly the farmer's wife who was the vintner, fitting the duty in with jam and pickle making. With the cost of imported wines being so great the less well-to-do took to winemaking to fulfil their needs. In many of Jane Austen's books you will read that they took pleasure in a glass of their home-made Elderberry wine.

The present boom can be traced back to the lifting of sugar rationing after the Second World War, and the fact that many of the returning troops had, whilst abroad, taken a fancy to wine drinking. This was coupled in latter years with the fact that travel abroad has become a way of life for all rather than for the few who, at one time, used to be the only ones who could afford it. There has been a great awakening interest in wine drinking, both home-made and that wine you buy which the home winemakers refer to as 'commercial wine'. With the help of technicians and the chemists the present-day winemaker has a much easier task in making first-class wine than his forebears. This is not to denigrate the earlier winemaking efforts, as many of our present standards are, in fact, a rationalisation and an improvement upon their basic principles.

In 1959 a monthly magazine *The Amateur Winemaker* was published and this was later followed by another magazine *Home Beer and Winemaker*. Wine Clubs have sprung up all over the country and provide a meeting point for those interested in the hobby. The clubs have formed into area federations who hold annual competitions and socials, and the top competition held annually is the 3-day conference and show run by the National Association of Amateur Winemakers.

The main body of wine judges is the Amateur Winemakers' National Guild of Judges. Most of the local authorities run evening classes on wine and beermaking. Interest in the hobby is growing weekly, and with the revived interest in making wine from wild fruits there has also been a revival of the growing of wine grapes in Great Britain to make a wine that can rival many of the Continental wines.

Basic equipment
With the great increase in foreign travel during the last decade, more and more people are discovering the delights of drinking wine. Unfortunately, during this period—and especially during the latter years—there has been a corresponding increase in wine prices. This has resulted in a great increase in interest in the ancient art of home-

made winemaking. It is to help those who are completely new to this hobby that I am writing this book on home-made wine and beer-making. Nonetheless, those who feel that they have a good knowledge of the subject may well find something to interest and inform them in this book.

Everyone who first takes up a hobby is interested in one vital fact: how much will it cost? Home winemaking is a hobby that requires very little outlay in equipment to make a modest gallon of wine, but this fact has been the downfall of many newcomers in that, having come into the hobby because of its little cost, they then become so price conscious that, having learnt the basics, they are very reluctant to spend any money at all upon their hobby and yet they still expect good results. As I have said, it costs very little for the basic equipment required to obtain a gallon of wine, so that you can with little cost get some idea as to whether you are going to enjoy the hobby. But once you have realised what an enjoyable hobby it is and how delightful the end product can be, you should then spend just a small amount of extra cash to equip yourself properly for winemaking on a rather larger scale.

All containers for wine should be made of glass or high density polythene. Avoid at all costs any type of metal containers unless they are made of stainless steel, which is not very likely due to their high cost. As polythene containers are so cheap, do not be tempted to use very old earthenware crocks as these may have had a lead glaze and their use for wine could cause serious poisoning. Saucepans for boiling ingredients are quite safe as the length of time the ingredients are in the saucepans will not cause any trouble. A 2-gallon pressure cooker used not as a pressure cooker but as an ordinary saucepan with the lid not sealed, is quite a useful saucepan.

For the storage of wine, during what is known as the fermenting period, the ideal vessel is the 1-gallon glass jar similar to the type that cider is sold in. These can be bought new from the wine equipment suppliers or, if you can obtain them, get those that have been used for cider or sauce, secondhand at half the price. The secondhand jars are quite safe to use once they have been thoroughly cleaned with bleach and then well washed out with cold water. You need at least 1 gallon jar to each gallon of wine you make, that is to say during the making period. You will also need a good supply of empty wine bottles ready for your finished wine. These can very easily be obtained from any hotel or club that has a licence—in fact they will be only too pleased to supply them to you as they do not have any return value. For corks for these bottles, obtain a supply of corks from your home-

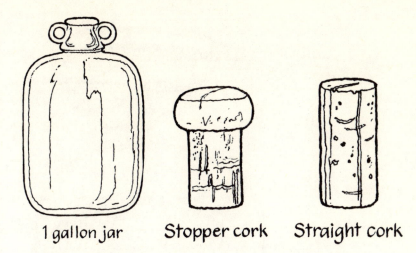

1 gallon jar   Stopper cork   Straight cork

made wine equipment supplier. The most convenient to use are the type known as stopper corks as these have a flange at the top and the cork can be taken out of the bottle and replaced without any damage to the stopper. Do not at any time use secondhand corks as this can very easily lead to infection in your wine.

You will need 2 funnels—one a large type with a diameter of at least 6 inches (8 inches is a good size), and a smaller funnel with a diameter of about 2 inches; the latter will be used to fill your wine bottles. For straining your ingredients you can either use a nylon sieve, which most households have, or you can purchase for a few

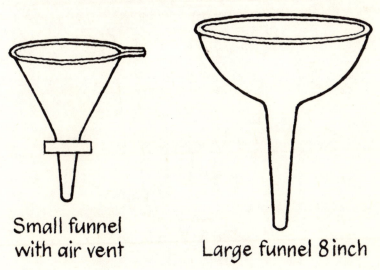

Small funnel
with air vent   Large funnel 8 inch

Small sieve

Cookery sieve

5 gallon fermentation
container

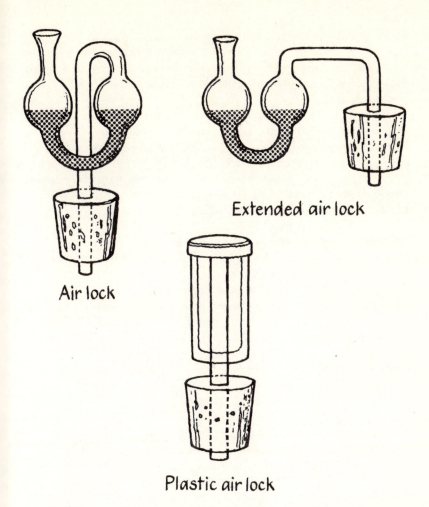

Air lock

Extended air lock

Plastic air lock

pence from your supplier a straining bag. For the early stages of your fermentation you require polythene buckets or dustbins. The latter are useful when making greater quantities than 1 gallon at a time but the raw beginner can get by quite easily with a 2-gallon bucket. However do not buy anything smaller than a 2-gallon bucket and —having purchased it—keep it solely for wine or beermaking.

The only other essential pieces of equipment are fermentation locks or, as they are sometimes called, air locks. These are very cheap and you need one for every gallon jar that you have. The last thing is a syphon tube. There are many types of syphons on sale which are very effective but for the newcomer I suggest that you buy 5 feet of clear polythene syphon tube with about a quarter inch inside diameter and into one end of the tube you can insert a glass U bend. The secret to this is to hold the end of the plastic tube in boiling water for about a minute, this soften the tube and you then find it quite a simple job to insert the straight end of the glass U bend into the heated end of your syphon tube.

As you will appreciate, I have only given the absolute minimum of equipment required to start winemaking. There are many more extras that can be added to this basic start once you have convinced yourself that winemaking is the hobby for you. Other articles, such as a hydrometer and jar, acid-testing equipment and larger containers and saucepans can, as I said, be increased as your enthusiasm for the hobby and your output of winemaking increases.

Glossary of terms used in winemaking

Base	The main ingredient from which a wine is made.
Body	Fullness or viscosity of a wine.
Campden Tablets	Tablets containing metabisulphite, used for sterilising a must, and inhibiting wild yeast.
Commercial Wine	Wine made professionally from wine grapes for sale at the wine merchants.
Carbon Dioxide	Colourless gas given off by fermentation.
Dry Wine	A wine without any sweetness and containing no residual sugar.
Fermentation	The conversion of sugar by yeast into alcohol and carbon dioxide gas.
Fermentation or Airlock	A glass or perspex container holding water which allows the carbon dioxide gas to escape whilst preventing air entering the gallon jar.
Fining	Added to wine to remove solids in a cloudy wine, thus making it clear.
Flowers of Wine	White powdery deposit forming on the surface of wine over-exposed to air.
Hydrometer	An instrument for measuring the amount of sugar in a liquid.
Hydrometer Jar	The vessel in which the wine is measured by means of floating the hydrometer in the wine.
Lees or Sediment	The waste deposit that collects in the bottom of a vessel containing fermenting wine.
Must	The name given to wine at the first stage when water and ingredients are brought together and yeast added.

Oxidisation	Browning of wine due to over-exposure to the air. Only desirable when making a sherry style wine.
Racking	The removal by syphoning of a wine from the lees.
Vitamin B1	Often sold under the trade name 'Aneurine'. One 3 mg. tablet per gallon.

Chapter 2
Making a Start

What is home-made wine?

The wine you buy is referred to by home winemakers as 'commercial wine' to differentiate it from the wines that they make. The commercial winemakers define their wine as the fermented juice of the freshly gathered grape. I think I should, for the benefit of the home winemakers, point out that the grapes the commercial makers use are a special variety of grape and you cannot successfully imitate them by the use of the dessert grapes that you buy from your greengrocer. The wine grape contains all the necessary acids, sugar and nutrients to make a successful wine, but their main problem is that in years when the weather is poor the sugar content of their grapes is sometimes too low, and in some wine-making countries the addition of sugar is sometimes not permitted. The home winemaker cannot, unless he lives in the southern half of England, grow wine grapes that are ripe enough to turn into wine. The result is that nearly all home-made wine is made from wild fruits or imported fruits other than grapes. Flowers, herbs, grains and vegetables can also be used to make an agreeable wine. Grape juice can be obtained in concentrate form but is usually the surplus and probably from the poorest crops of the grape-producing countries. Grape juice wine made from these concentrates cannot rival the wines made from the fresh grape juice.

The ingredient base fruits, flowers, vegetables or grains from which we make our home-made wine lack some of the essential minerals that the wine grape has, so to overcome this we have to make additions of acids, tannin and nutrients to our wines to aid fermentation. Fortunately these are very cheap and easily obtained. As a result we can make very pleasant wines which have a flavour and character of their own and they are none the worse for that. The secret to all home winemaking is to obtain a balance between all the ingredients so that they marry together to produce a smooth wine that is neither too sweet, too dry, too full-flavoured or too harsh, and it is here that a good recipe is of such great help.

Before going any further it is important to understand what wine is when you get down to basics. From the home winemaker's point of view it is a sweetened liquid which has a flavour to which a yeast has been added. The yeast then commences to ferment and in effect it consumes the sugar in the solution and produces alcohol. When this has happened, the result is wine. Before we can progress any further it is necessary to deal with yeasts and their importance.

Yeasts

Yeast is the engine room of winemaking and it is its action on sugar solutions that produces the required alcohol. It is microscopic but in the correct medium each cell multiplies itself many thousand times in an hour. In the early days of winemaking the only form of yeast available was Bakers Yeast. This produces the alcohol quite readily but often imparts a 'bready' off-flavour in the wine. Even today some winemakers still think that this is the most reliable form. These days nearly every town or village has its own home winemaking supplier where you can obtain wine yeast in either dried or liquid form. When purchased the yeast is in an inert form and needs to be activated at least three days prior to making your wine. To reproduce, the yeast needs the correct medium which is water, sugar, yeast nutrients and yeast food, all mixed and kept at the correct temperature of 70°F. To do this you make what is known as a Yeast Starter Bottle. Before I explain how this is done, let us discuss the two ingredients that I have mentioned but not explained, namely yeast nutrients and yeast food. These are two of the ingredients that are found naturally in wine grapes but which are missing from the fruits and bases that we have to make our wine from.

Yeast Nutrients

These are sold as yeast nutrient tablets and are either ammonium sulphate or ammonium phosphate. This adds nitrogen salts that assist the yeast cells to multiply. The beginner would be well advised to buy the tablet form, the usual addition being 1 tablet per gallon.

Yeast Food

This is a vitamin addition and adds Vitamin B1 which also helps in the fermentation, especially when you wish to produce a high amount of alcohol. These are sold by the suppliers under various trade names or can be purchased from Boots the Chemists under the trade name 'Aneurine' (3 milligramme tablets) quite cheaply. Here again you add one tablet per gallon of wine.

Yeast Starter Bottle

Three days before you commence to make your wine you should prepare your starter bottle. Take a thoroughly cleaned milk bottle and pour half a pint of cold water into it. Then add 1 yeast nutrient tablet and one 3 mg Aneurine tablet. Then add 4 teaspoonsful of granulated sugar. Place the palm of your hand over the bottle mouth and shake until all the ingredients have dissolved. Stand the bottle in a warm place at about 70°F and put a piece of cotton wool in the mouth of the bottle to keep out flies and dirt. After about 24 hours the solution should start to go milky and by the third day bubbles can be seen to be rising in the bottle which means the yeast is rapidly increasing in numbers. The yeast starter is now full of active yeast and when added to the *Must*, as the wine is called in its early stages, the yeast will immediately start the fermentation. Failure to make a yeast starter means that your must would take longer to start the fermentation with the danger of turning to vinegar. It is advisable to make a new yeast starter with a new yeast for every wine that you make. The yeasts are sold under various commercial wine varieties, e.g. Burgundy, Sauterne and so on. From experience, I have found little to be gained by using the different varieties and prefer the type called General Purpose yeast. Do not think that because you have used a Burgundy yeast it will make your wine taste like a Burgundy. The only two types of yeasts that are necessary for special wines are, I feel, Sherry Yeast and Champagne Yeast.

Additives

Tannin

This is one of the most important additives yet is neglected by many winemakers. Tannin, which comes from grape stalks and pips, fulfils several purposes. It assists in maintaining the colour of a wine. It is slightly antiseptic against bacteria. It helps in the final clearing of a wine and, last but not least, gives wine the characteristic 'bite'. Without tannin the wine would be too soft and flabby. There is no easy way to determine the tannin content of a wine so rule-of-thumb has to be used. Tannin is required in all flower and herb wines. It is also required in all white wines but most red wines obtain enough tannin from the red skins of the fruit, so additives are not usually necessary. The normal addition of tannin to a wine is half a teaspoonful per gallon of wine. It can be obtained from your wine equipment supplier.

Pectin

Pectin is a natural substance found to a greater or lesser degree in all fruits and vegetables. This is the substance that causes fruit when boiled for a long period to go stiff and turn into jam. The effect on wine is to make it cloudy and impossible to clear without special treatment. To avoid this happening it is better to treat the must with a pectin-destroying enzyme at the outset of making the wine. This is sold under various trade names such as Pectinex, Pectinol and similar names, with full instructions on how to use it. The treatment does not affect the taste of the wine in any way and is quite safe to use. Avoid over-boiling any fruit or vegetables as this will produce an excess of pectin that will be difficult to remove. Pectin-removing substances also have an additional use in that, if put into the must at the outset, they help in the breakdown of the fruit, which gives a higher yield of extract.

Rohament P
This is obtained from suppliers and should be used when making wine from fleshy fruit such as apples, peaches, apricots, etc., as it assists greatly in breaking down the cellular walls of the fruit and gives a much greater extract per pound of fruit. It should be added at the rate of 2–5 gms (2 level teaspoonsful of Rohament P to every 3 kgs (6 lbs) of fruit per gallon). Make sure that any addition of acid is made before adding the Rohament P. The Rohament P should be added to the must when it is at room temperature 68°F (20°C).

Acidity
Acid plays a very important part in winemaking. Every wine must have an acid content. If the wine must does not have sufficient acid you will have trouble in getting the wine to ferment and the finished product will have a flat medicinal taste.

Nonetheless it must be remembered that too little acid is better than too much acid. If the acid content of the finished wine is a little too low, extra acid can be added without spoiling the wine. If you have too much acid in the finished wine it is more difficult to remove without leaving an unpleasant taste.

If you have a wine that is too acid, it is better to reduce the acidity by blending it with a wine that is low in acid.

The acid generally used by winemakers to add acidity to the must is citric acid. This is a white powder and should be kept in an airtight container. Other acids that can be used are malic acid which is found in apples and tartaric acid which is in high concentration in grapes. One good feature of the use of tartaric acid is that if your finished wine is a little too acid, chilling the wine at low temperature will cause crystals to precipitate on to the bottom of the container. These crystals are quite harmless and are, in fact, cream of tartar. When the wine is decanted off the crystals the acidity of the wine will be decreased.

The only exact way to determine the acidity of the must is by means of a pH meter. These are extremely expensive, so they are out of the reckoning. It is possible to determine the acidity by means of a titration kit. These can be bought from your wine suppliers, complete with full instructions and measurement tables. They cost under £1 and are quite simple to use. There is only one drawback to their use and that is that the readings they give can be slightly misleading as they give the total acidity. In some cases the total acidity will create the impression that the wine or must is slightly more acid than it actually is. This is not altogether a bad fault. By using the titration kit correctly you will get an acidity that is nearly correct. If, when tasting the finished wine, it is slightly low in acid you can always add a little extra acid.

Bases with low acidity	Bases with medium acidity	Bases with high acidity
Elderberries	Pomegranates	Blackcurrants
All flowers	Apricots	Blackberries
Bananas	Loganberries	Citrus fruits—
Pears	Dessert cherries	oranges, lemons,
Dates	Foreign dessert	tangerines,
Honey	grapes	grapefruit
Figs	Bilberries	Plums
Dried rose hips	Strawberries	Raspberries
Currants	Grape concentrate	Gooseberries
Raisins	Apples	Cooking cherries
Sultanas		Rhubarb
Herbs		Sloes
		Pineapple
		Crab apples

Additions of acid by 'rule-of-thumb':
Low acid base—2 teaspoonsful citric acid.
Medium acid base—1 teaspoonful citric acid.
High acid base—add no acid.
Tartaric acid can be used instead of citric acid.

The titration kit is popular because with the great variety of bases it is difficult to judge whether a must is going to be a high acid or low acid must. Beginners may not wish to spend on the cost of a kit at the outset of their winemaking but there is a remedy to avoid this. This is called 'rule-of-thumb'. You decide from your own knowledge of the base from which you are making your wine whether it is a high acid base or a low one. If it is high in acid do not add any extra acid. If it is a low acid base then add one teaspoonful of citric or tartaric acid to the must. To assist you, on page 23 is a table showing many of the bases from which wine is made, indicating whether it is low, medium or high in acid. The only other factor that you have to take into account is the quantity of the base you are using in your recipe. For example, gooseberries are high in acid but if you were using a recipe that only required 1 pound of gooseberries then you would need to add acid; but if you were using a recipe with 3 pounds of gooseberries you would not need to add any acid.

The main thing to remember is that it is easier to add acid to a wine than to remove it.

Sterilisation
No winemaker will ever succeed—no matter how skilful—unless he ensures cleanliness at every stage of the operation. Bacteria is always present and only constant vigilance and use of sterilisation will keep it at bay. With a little bit of organisation and cleanliness at every stage, the problem is diminished to such an extent that it will no longer be a problem. The two main ways of sterilisation are by heat or chemical treatment. The first method of heat is not very practicable, so the universally accepted method is by use of chemical agents.

Many proprietary powders are sold to make up into a sterilisation solution and use as directed. If you wish to make up your own, the chemical to buy from your chemist or winemaking supplier is sodium metabisulphite. This can be bought cheaply in bulk, say 1 lb. (450 gms approx.). It can also be bought in the form of Campden tablets. If bought in bulk as sodium metabisulphite it should be kept in an airtight container or it will lose its strength. A stock sterilisation solution is to dissolve 5 ozs of metabisulphite in 1 gallon of water and keep in a sealed glass container (100 gms to 3 litres). Equipment should be submerged in this solution for about one hour, and drained, then it is ready for use. Household bleach can also be used at the rate of 2 fluid ozs to 1 gallon of water (56 ml to $4\frac{1}{2}$ litres), but remember that after sterilisation your equipment must be well washed in cold water before use.

The must can be sterilised by the addition of 2 Campden tablets to each gallon, added 24 hours before the addition of the yeast. Campden tablets should only be added when the must is cold.

To clean badly stained gallon jars or bottles, add a little pure bleach, swill around and brush inside with a bottle brush. Remember to wash out well with plenty of cold water to remove all traces of bleach before use.

Chapter 3
The Fermentation Process

Fermentation is the conversion of the sugar solution flavoured by your fruits into alcohol. The initial fermentation which lasts 2 to 3 weeks is very vigorous and gives the appearance of boiling water, and when stirred you can hear the hiss from the rising bubbles. The second stage of fermentation is much slower and not so spectacular and can last for several months. The act of fermentation is when the contents of the yeast starter bottle are added to your sweetened fruit juices and the yeast feeds on the sugar, converting it roughly into 2 halves. One half is given off in carbon dioxide gas and the other half is converted into alcohol. A word of warning: to ensure that your fermentation gets off to a good start, do not add too much sugar into your must at the first stage. If the recipe requires 3 lbs of sugar to the gallon of wine, then only add 2 of the 3 pounds of sugar at the start and add the other 1 lb. after the wine has been fermenting for several weeks. Adding the 3 lbs at the outset may cause the fermentation to be slow or even to stop altogether.

The initial week of the first fermentation can take place in an open vessel such as a 2-gallon plastic bucket or plastic dustbin of 5 gallon capacity for making more than 1 gallon at a time. The ideal temperature for fermentation is around 70°F. It is not always possible to maintain this temperature and when the temperature drops the fermentation will slow down but will pick up again as the temperature rises again. Too high a fermentation around 85°F may kill the yeast. Too cold a temperature will only slow it down. Nonetheless, if possible, try and keep the fermentation as near as possible to a steady 70°F.

As the fermentation proceeds, the sugar content of the solution decreases and the alcohol content increases. In theory, the more sugar you add, the more the yeast will consume it and the higher the volume of alcohol which will be produced. Unfortunately, in practice, this is not so, as there is a limit to the amount of alcohol that you can produce. Nature seems to work hand in glove with the Customs and Excise Department! It must be remembered that yeasts are living organisms and, like human beings, some are more vigorous than others and some can do more work than others—and again like human beings—they thrive best in an ideal atmosphere. Although some winemakers make extravagant claims about the amount of alcohol that they produce, the general opinion is that a very good yeast in ideal conditions will ferment out 3 half-pounds of sugar in a gallon of water and produce about 18% by volume of alcohol. This is roughly between 31% and 32% proof—nearly half the strength of whisky. But remember it is not always possible to obtain these high results as some yeasts stop fermenting well below the figures quoted.

Sugar

Many winemakers, when reading books containing old-fashioned recipes, are worried by the continual use of candy sugar or preserving sugar chips. There is no extra value to be obtained in using these types of sugar, even if you can get them, and, in any case, they are more expensive. The best type of sugar to use is the normal white granulated sugar on sale at all grocers. This is the cheapest and is just as sweet as candy sugar or preserving sugar. Brown or Demerara sugar can be used in those recipes which require colouring, with a slight rum flavour, but in all other wines use granulated. There is a sugar used mainly by brewers called invert sugar. This is a normal granulated sugar that has been boiled in slight acid solution. This process inverts the sugar. When you use granulated sugar the yeast does the process of invertion for you but to do this before converting sugar to alcohol takes up several hours and the fermentation using invert sugar starts just that little bit more quickly than with granulated sugar. In beermaking, especially on the commercial level, time is money, but for the home winemaker the very slight gain in time by the use of invert sugar is greatly offset by its much higher cost. So, as I have said, use granulated sugar. Some winemakers when making additions of sugar to their wines like to add the sugar in the form of a sugar solution. This solution is made by boiling until it clarifies. Use 1 lb. of sugar in half a pint of water and allow to go cold before adding to the wine. A word of warning if you adopt this system: do not make a stock sugar solution as this is the ideal medium for harmful bacteria to thrive in and the addition of an infected sugar solution will cause faults in your wine.

If you are adding sugar in solution, make up a fresh solution for every addition to your wine. I have always added sugar to the wine in its dry state. Stirring with a wooden spoon only takes about 5 minutes before all the sugar is dissolved, even in a cold liquid. When adding sugar to a wine it is better to add too little than too much. Remember, you can always add further sugar if required but if you add too much sugar you cannot remove it from your wine and you will finish up with a wine that is too sweet.

The amount of sugar used in making a wine has a direct bearing on the amount of alcohol in the finished wine. Any sugar left in a wine when it has finished fermenting is called residual sugar and the amount of this residual sugar decides whether the wine is sweet, and how sweet. A dry wine is a wine that does not have any residual sugar. In early books on winemaking it was very popular to pick on a particular fruit to make a wine from, and by adding 2 lbs of sugar it was made into a dry wine, i.e. unsweetened. Then, by using the same recipe but this time adding $3\frac{1}{2}$ lbs of sugar, the same wine was made into a sweet wine. Modern thinking amongst winemakers have progressed from this point of view. It is now realised that certain bases, (that is to say what the wine is made from) lend themselves to a particular type of wine. An example of this is apples, which are a delicate flavoured fruit and make a much better dry wine than a sweet wine. When made into a sweet wine the sugar remaining in the wine overcomes the flavour of the fruit and when you drink the wine you only taste the sugar and not the flavour of the fruit. Broadly speaking, strong flavoured fruits lend themselves more to the making of sweet wine and delicate flavoured fruit are more suitable to dry wines. Like all generalisations, there are exceptions to the rule.

The recipes in Chapter 8 have been selected so that the base used is the one most suitable to the type of wine aimed for.

The hydrometer and how to use it
The hydrometer is the most useful piece of equipment that the winemaker has. Unfortunately, so many new winemakers fight shy of learning how to use it. It is a very simple piece of equipment and is really no more difficult to use than a thermometer to take a sick person's temperature. It shows how much sugar there is in the ingredients with which you are making your wine. With this amount known you are able to determine how much sugar in the form of granulated sugar you need to add to your must. You will remember that I stated that the yeast when it ferments in a must, consumes the sugar in the must. The hydrometer enables you to find out how the fermentation is progressing and, also, how much sugar to add to the must. From the amount of sugar consumed by the yeast you can work out the approximate amount of alcohol in your finished wine.

A word of warning though: when you buy your hydrometer do not be tempted into making use of a milk bottle or similar container as a measuring jar. They will not be deep enough, so ensure that you buy a hydrometer *and* hydrometer jar. The hydrometer is a glass tube scaled into a bulbous end. It is fairly fragile, so handle it with care. When measuring the sugar content of a liquid, place the hydrometer into the hydrometer jar and pour the liquid gently into the jar. Do not put the liquid into the jar first and then lower the hydrometer in as it may hit the bottom and break. The scale on the inside of the stem of the hydrometer is arranged so that water has a Specific Gravity of 1·000. Specific Gravity is the term used to describe the viscosity of the liquid, the denser it is, the higher will be the Specific Gravity reading. You can test this by measuring the S.G. of your hydrometer jar containing cold water and then dissolving 2 ozs of sugar into the same liquid. Then upon re-testing you will see that the S.G. has increased.

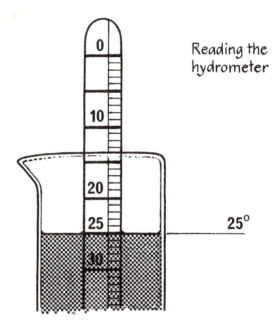

Reading the hydrometer

From this you will appreciate that the hydrometer measures the sugar content of a liquid. Always measure the S.G. when the liquid is cold as you will appreciate the warmer the liquid the thinner it is.

A further example of S.G. readings: 1 lb sugar dissolved and made up to 1 gallon of liquid gives a S.G. of 1·040. The same gallon of water without sugar reads 1·000. You will notice that the figure '1' before the decimal point is constant and remains constant throughout all our readings, so for ease we dispense with it. The reading of water is now S.G. '0' and the reading of 1 lb of sugar dissolved and made up to 1 gallon reads S.G. '40'. It is bad winemaking policy to add all the sugar required by a recipe to the must at the outset, particularly if it is a high alcohol recipe. It is the same as giving a baby a piece of steak— it will probably choke upon it. But the baby could probably eat the same piece of steak if cut up and given a bit at a time. The same principle, to a lesser degree, is apparent with yeast in a sugar solution.

If you put 3 lbs of sugar into a must and make the quantity up to a gallon of wine, the yeast may either fail to start, or stop fermentation before all the sugar has been consumed. Remember I said the yeast is a living organism and some consume more sugar than others. The 3 lbs of sugar made into a gallon of must has a S.G. of 115. Rather than start at this figure I would advise adding sufficient sugar to the must to raise the S.G. to 70. Ferment this to dryness, i.e. S.G. 0, then add sufficient sugar to raise the S.G. to 45, and you will find that the yeast can cope quite easily with sugar at these rates. When you approach the S.G. of 115 you are getting close to the maximum that some yeasts can go, and further additions of sugar after the yeast has consumed 115 S.G. may not all be consumed. Any sugar left in the wine is called residual sugar which will remain as a sweetening agent. My suggestion is to approach 115 S.G. by two stages: S.G. 70 ferment to dryness; add sugar to raise S.G. to 45 (approximately 19 ozs) and again ferment to dryness S.G. 0. From this point on you only raise the S.G. to the figure that you wish the wine to finish at—that is to say if you wish to make a wine with a finished sweetness of S.G. 10 then, the yeast having consumed 115 S.G. by two stages (S.G. 70 and S.G. 45), you raise the S.G. by adding sugar to give an S.G. of 10 and every time the yeast consumes these $10°$ of gravity, raise it again to 10. The yeast will eventually stop fermenting because the alcohol content is so high that it can no longer ferment in such an atmosphere. You then only need to add sufficient sugar to bring the S.G. to 10 and you have a finished wine at the degree of sweetness that you require.

To take the S.G. of a must, just prior to adding the contents of your yeast starter bottle, strain a hydrometer jar full of the liquid through a strainer and take the reading. Then add sufficient sugar to raise the S.G. to 70 and proceed as suggested. Dry table wines may be commenced with an S.G. of between 85 and 90 and fermented to dryness and no further additions of sugar are required.

Always record the S.G. figures with date on all occasions when you add sugar to your wine. Add together the amounts of S.G. consumed by the yeast and, after subtracting the final S.G. of the wine, you will then have the full amount of S.G. consumed by the wine. By referring to the alcohol tables you will be able to ascertain the percentage of alcohol by volume. If you multiply that figure by 7 and divide it by 4 you will have the approximate strength in terms of proof spirit. For a guide as to strength, the average proprietary whisky is 70% proof.

A Typical Specific Gravity Reading of a Wine
Wine required: sweet wine with a finished Specific Gravity of 10.
Wine commenced

  1.6.73 S.G. 70
20.6.73 S.G. 0   Sugar added S.G. 45
  1.7.73 S.G. 0   Sugar added S.G. 10
12.7.73 S.G. 0   Sugar added S.G. 10
  1.8.73 S.G. 5   wine ceased
                            fermentation at this
                            point

Sugar added to raise finished S.G. to 10
The addition of the S.G. used up equals

              70 to 0 = 70
              45 to 0 = 45
              10 to 0 = 10
              10 to 0 = 10
              10 to 5 = 5

           Total S.G. used   = 140

S.G. 140 19 —4% by volume. This figure multiplied by 7 and divided by 4—33·9% proof spirit.

The times of fermentation vary from wine to wine and the above figures represent the maximum alcohol that can normally be obtained.

Specific Gravity Tables

S.G.	Potential % Alcohol	Amount of sugar in one gallon	Amount of sugar added to one gallon
10	0·9	2 ozs (57 gms)	2½ ozs (71 gms)
15	1·6	4 ozs (114 gms)	5 ozs (142 gms)
20	2·3	7 ozs (199 gms)	8 ozs (228 gms)
25	3·0	9 ozs (256 gms)	10 ozs (284 gms)
30	3·7	12 ozs (341 gms)	13 ozs (369 gms)
35	4·4	15 ozs (426 gms)	1 lb (454 gms)
40	5·1	1 lb 1 oz (482 gms)	1 lb 2 ozs (511 gms)
45	5·8	1 lb 3 ozs (539 gms)	1 lb 4 ozs (567 gms)
50	6.5	1 lb 5 ozs (596 gms)	1 lb 7 ozs (653 gms)
55	7·2	1 lb 7 ozs (653 gms)	1 lb 9 ozs (709 gms)
60	7·8	1 lb 9 ozs (709 gms)	1 lb 11 ozs (766 gms)
65	8·6	1 lb 11 ozs (766 gms)	1 lb 14 ozs (851 gms)
70	9·2	1 lb 13 ozs (823 gms)	2 lb 1 oz (937 gms)
75	9·9	1 lb 15 ozs (879 gms)	2 lb 4 ozs (1 kg)

80	10·6	2 lb 1 oz (937 gms)	2 lb 6 ozs (1 kg 57 gms)
90	12	2 lb 6 ozs (1 kg 57 gms)	2 lb 12 ozs (1 kg 227 gms)
95	12·7	2 lb 8 ozs (1 kg 114 gms)	2 lb 15 ozs (1 kg 312 gms)
100	13·4	2 lb 10 ozs (1 kg 171 gms)	3 lb 2 ozs (1 kg 397 gms)
110	14·9	2 lb 14 ozs (1 kg 285 gms)	3 lb 8 ozs (1 kg 589 gms)
120	16·3	3 lb 2 ozs (1 kg 397 gms)	3 lb 14 ozs (1 kg 759 gms)
130	17·7	3 lb 6 ozs (1 kg 533 gms)	4 lb 4 ozs (1 kg 930 gms)

Temperature control

It has been a common error amongst home winemakers that a slow, long fermentation is good for wine. I do not believe this to be true. The commercial winemakers do not have wines fermenting a long time and certainly not as long as some home winemakers try to achieve. Yeast works best in an even temperature and when wine is in the gallon jars under the kitchen table you can get a great fluctuation in temperature. Take a home that does not have central heating: during the winter the family will be out all day and the room quite cold. In the evening the room will be heated and then when the family have gone to bed the temperature of the room will rapidly fall. This continuing fluctuation does not help the yeast.

The ideal answer is a fermentation cupboard. You need a cupboard with the space between the shelves sufficient to take the height of a gallon jar plus the air lock. Sometimes the extended airlock rather than the upright type can make all the difference between a cupboard being usable or too small. If you have a cupboard into which you can fit your gallon jars, line the walls and inside of the doors with polystyrene paper and fit strip sponge rubber around the edges of the doors to avoid heat loss. In the cupboard suspend a 100 watt light into which is linked a thermostat set at 70°F (21°C). The thermostat can be purchased quite cheaply from your equipment supplier. The better you insulate your cupboard the cheaper it will be to heat. In this way you can ferment your wines at an even temperature and there will be less chance of sticking fermentations.

If you do not have a suitable cupboard, a tea chest lined and insulated and heated with a 100 watt lamp linked with a thermostat will keep 5 one-gallon jars at an even temperature of 70°F. For safety, the lamp should be in an open-ended tin such as a dried milk tin. To assist with insulation cover the tea chest with an old blanket or blankets. If well insulated by this method you can keep 5 gallons of wine at 70°F for as little as 5p per week. When not in use for wine it can be used for your beer bottles after priming to get the beer gassy.

Chapter 4
Base Materials for Home-made Wine

Extracting flavour from your base

Wine can be made from a variety of base materials which differ greatly in their structure, and so different methods are used to obtain the flavour from these varying bases. The main methods of extraction are:

1. Fermenting on the pulp
2. Boiling
3. By mechanical means
   a) Juice extractors
   b) Pressing

Fermenting on the Pulp

This is by far the most popular method of extraction for soft fruits. The fruit to be used as your base is either crushed by hand or cut up, depending on whether the fruit is soft or firm. It is then placed into your open fermenting vessel and treated with Rohament P, pectin-destroying enzyme and Campden tablets. The Campden tablets are added at the rate of 2 to 3 to each gallon of wine to be made. The more ripe the fruit, the higher the number of Campden tablets to be used.

To the fruit is added your cold water. Generally if you are making a gallon of wine it is preferable to add only 6 pints ($3\frac{1}{2}$ litres). The addition of sugar and the juice from the fruit will increase the quantity of liquid, and any addition of cold water to make up the gallon can be made after straining.

A cover is placed over the fermenting vessel and the fruit pulp, water and pectin-destroying enzyme, Campden tablets, acid and Rohament P are left for 24 hours before the addition of the sugar, contents of yeast starter bottle and other ingredients. Stir well and ferment on the pulp for at least 3 days. It is easy to see if the pulp is fermenting as the fruit pulp will rise to the top and, when stirred, the liquid will hiss and bubble just as if it was boiling.

After the 3 days of fermentation the liquid and pulp should be squeezed by hand through a straining bag (these can be purchased cheaply from equipment suppliers). When dealing with red fruit, such as elderberries, ladies may wish to wear rubber gloves as the juice may stain their hands and take several days to wear off.

Having strained off your liquid you can now make any addition of sugar water to bring your quantity up to the amount specified in the recipe. The liquid is now poured into a gallon jar (glass) and a fermentation lock and cork is inserted. To insert the airlock into the gallon jar stopper, soak the cork for a few minutes in hot water (the lock will be easy to insert into the cork stopper). A small quantity of water can be put into the air lock, the cap replaced and the wine can now be placed into a warm atmosphere to continue fermentation 70°F (21°C) if possible.

Boiling

Some winemakers like to boil their fruit before fermenting on the pulp. The fruit most frequently treated in this way is elderberry. It certainly extracts the maximum amount of colour. The fruit is boiled in a quantity of water for about 20 minutes. The liquid and pulp is then poured into the fermentation vessel and, when cold, more water is added. The must is then treated as for fermentation on the pulp. There will be a slight difference in the flavour of wines made this way. The difference will be appreciated when you realise the difference in, say, a fresh apple and a stewed apple. It is all a matter of personal taste.

The main use of the boiling method is for the treatment of vegetables. Before boiling any vegetables, wash them and cut them up into fairly equally sized pieces. The vegetables can then be boiled in a quantity of water. Do not over-boil as this will cause pectin haze and over-boiling will make it very difficult to clear the eventual wine. The vegetables should be boiled until they can just be pierced with a fork. The liquid is then strained off and the other ingredients added and the quantity made up with cold water. Remember that the yeast starter bottle contents must only be added when the must is cold.

Mechanical Means

The wine press is a very popular means of extracting the juice from grapes and very soft fruits. The larger the press, the better and easier to use. One disadvantage is that with the smaller type of press usually used by home winemakers the fruit has to be preliminarily crushed or broken by hand before putting into a bag and placing into the wine press. From experience I find that squeezing by hand is quicker and more effective.

Steam extractors can be bought whereby the fruit is cut up and placed in a steamer. Here again you get the danger of extracting too much pectin which will cause clearing problems.

We now come to the electrical juice extractors. To name a few:

Kenwood, Moulinex, Beekay—and the one I have used very success-fully—the Vitamine. The electrical extractors come with full instruc-tions and are very easy to use. Anyone wishing to extract juice from vegetables such as carrots, that are not really suitable for the electrical extractor, should purchase a Jumbo Juicer. This is similar to a large hand mincer; the juice comes out at the front and the pulp comes out at the back. I have used this very effectively on carrots, which I think are one of the best vegetables to make wine from.

Two base ingredients that I have not yet mentioned are dried herbs and flower petals. The herbs should be simmered for about 20 minutes in a quantity of water and, after simmering, the liquid and dried herbs are poured into the fermenting vessel and treated as for fermenting on the pulp.

Flower petals make a very pleasant wine but it must be re-membered that only flowers that have a scent are of any use for wine-making. With coloured petals, pour a quantity of boiling water over the petals and allow to stand for half an hour, then strain off and add liquid to fermentation vessel. Make up quantity of water and add other ingredients. The use of boiling water on the petals will ensure that you get a good colour-extraction without any loss of bouquet or flavour. Hot or cold water may be used in the case of white petals.

Choosing the correct base
For too long home winemakers have been making wine under a false premise. Early writers upon the subject advocated that wine can be made from windfalls and any old fruit irrespective of quality. It was also suggested that whatever fruit that happened to be in season could be successfully turned into any style of wine. By 'style of wine' I am referring to whether the wine is a dry wine, table wine, sweet wine, dessert wine or aperitif. There is a difference between a dry wine and a table wine. A dry wine should have a fair amount of flavour and body but should be dry. That is to say, it should not have any residual sweetness. It can also have as much alcohol as you desire.

A table wine should not be too full-flavoured or have too much alcohol as in the first instance when taken with food, the flavour of the wine will smother the taste of the food and, in the latter, you will find that if too high in alcohol you will be feeling the effects of this before the meal is finished. A table wine should be dry and not have fermented any more than a total S.G. of 1·100.

A sweet wine should be full-bodied and full-flavoured and, in the case of dessert wine, should be fairly high in alcohol. The secret of winemaking is to create a balance of the qualities, of a balance of tannin, alcohol, flavour, acidity, body and bouquet.

As regards the most suitable base to use, one point is abundantly clear if we look at the commercial winemakers. Take one of the top Claret Châteaux, such as Mouton Rothschilds. They use the same vines in the same soil with the same husbandry and cellar-craft each year. One years will only produce a reasonable wine whereas another year will produce a simply marvellous wine. This is due entirely to one thing—the weather. When the rain and sun come in the right quantities at the right time, the resultant crop produces a magnificent wine. The same can be said of the wine made from fruit grown in our own country, and the same yardstick should be applied. For example, if we have a poor cold, wet, summer the wild fruits will be high in acid and lacking in flavour, and no matter how you treat such fruit it will not make a good wine. It is more difficult when dealing with fruit grown abroad as you will not know what their season has been. In the case of fruit bases that can be tasted (obviously elderberry is not one of these), taste the fruit. If it is not full-flavoured when you taste it, turning it into wine will not suddenly endow it with qualities it did not have when you tasted it. Get the best quality fruits available to turn into wine. Avoid unripened or damaged fruit.

We must again refer to the commercial wine world to amplify the next point. In the commercial world you will find that certain grape varieties are used to make a certain style of wine. For example, the grapes grown in Burgundy are only used to make a table wine, not a dessert wine. In the same way, the fruits we use to make home-made wines lend themselves to a particular style of wine. A light-flavoured fruit should only be made into a table wine. Any attempt to make it into a dessert wine will result in failure as the amount of residual sugar will override and smother the flavour. For light delicate wines only use a base with a light delicate flavour.

Many winemakers mistakenly make wine from dessert grapes bought from the greengrocer with the thought that all grapes can be turned into a good wine. Unfortunately this is not the case. Commercial wine is made from wine grapes which are quite different from dessert grapes and thus the use of dessert grapes only produces a very indifferent wine. There is an exception to this as there is for most rules. I find that the seedless sultana grapes from Cyprus—usually in the shops during September—make a reasonable table wine and a very good sparkling wine.

The quantities of the fruit used in the main base of your wines will also vary according to the style of wine to be made. For a table wine— 2 lbs to 3 lbs (1 kilo to 1½ kilos); for a dessert wine—4 lbs (2 kilos), and upwards of fruit per gallon.

The following is a list of some of the fresh fruit bases that wine can be made from, and the style of wine to which they are best suited:

Table Wine	Dry Wine	Sweet Wine	Dessert Wine
Apple	Apple	—	—
Apricot	Apricot	—	—
Blackberry (cultivated)	Blackberry (wild)	Blackberry (wild)	Blackberry (wild)
—	—	Banana	Banana
Bilberry	Bilberry	—	—
Blackcurrant	Blackcurrant	Blackcurrant	Blackcurrant
Cherry (Morello)	Cherry (Morello)	Cherry (Morello)	Cherry (Morello)
Cherry (red and white)	Cherry (red and white)	—	—
Currant (red and white)	Currant (red and white)	—	—
Damson	Damson	Damson	Damson
Elderberry	Elderberry	Elderberry	Elderberry
Gooseberry	Gooseberry	Gooseberry (Dessert)	—
Grapefruit	Grapefruit	Grapefruit	Grapefruit
—	Loganberry	Loganberry	Loganberry
—	Orange	Orange	Orange
Peach	Peach	Peach	—
—	Plum	Plum	Plum
—	Rose Hip	Rose Hip	—
Quince	Quince	—	—
—	Raspberry	Raspberry	Raspberry
—	Strawberry	Strawberry	Strawberry
—	Tangerine	Tangerine	Tangerine

Flower Wines

Many pleasant wines are made from flower petals but it must be remembered that the only thing you can extract from the petals is the bouquet. The tannin—body and acidity, etc.—must be added. It follows from this that the only flower petals that are of any use are from flowers with a strong bouquet. If you use flowers without a scent the wine will be tasteless. The ideal flower is the rose. Such varieties as 'Fragrant Cloud', 'Wendy Cussons', 'Ena Harkness' and 'Crimson Glory' are ideal for this purpose.

Another popular flower is the elderflower. Wines from this flower can either be a success or a disaster. Some of these petals have a strong 'catty' bouquet. Use of petals with this scent will make a terrible wine. Search carefully for an elder bush with petals with a delicate musky flavour and you will be surprised how delightful this wine can be, especially served chilled with a slice of lemon. To all flower wines add tannin, acid and either minced sultanas or white grape concentrate to give the wine body. Yeast nutrient and vitamin B1 additive should also be included.

Wines from other bases

There are many bases from which wine can be made. One of the best of these is fresh parsley. With the addition of a little lemon peel (peel minus any pith) this makes a delightful drink. Wine from dried herbs makes another addition to the list of bases: usually about 2 ozs (60 gms approx) per gallon. Here again additions must be made for tannin, acid, yeast nutrient, vitamin B1, and either sultanas or grape concentrate to give body.

Vegetable Wines

The only vegetables I would recommend for wine are parsnips and carrots. The flavour should be extracted by boiling. Before boiling, cut the vegetables into pieces of as near as possible to equal size. Do not overboil and add pectic enzyme to the must.

Grain Wines

There is a mistaken idea amongst some winemakers that wines made from grain such as rice, wheat or barley makes a stronger alcoholic drink than wines from a fruit base. The strength of a wine depends solely upon the amount of sugar converted by the yeast into alcohol. Wines from a grain base tend to give a wine which burns the throat when swallowed and this is often mistaken for alcoholic strength. I have included several recipes for this type of wine although I would not recommend them when there are so many fruits available from which a much superior wine can be made. The best of the grain wines is barley, but this must not be confused with the strong ale sometimes called barley wine.

Dried Fruits
During the winter when many of the fresh fruits are not available, many interesting wines can be made from dried fruit. They will be different in flavour from their fresh fruit counterparts in the same way that dried pears reconstituted and stewed have a different taste to fresh stewed pears. The thing to remember is that you need much less dried fruit to the equivalent wine made from fresh fruit. The most striking example is dried elderberry which only requires ½ lb (226 gms) to make a gallon of wine.

Tinned Fruit
Another welcome addition to wine bases for our off-season wine-making are the large tins of fruit usually about 6 lbs (3 kilos approx). These are often catering packs and usually the fruit is unsweetened. Two particular tins I have tried, with excellent results, are goose-berries and Morello cherries. The wine made from Morello cherries was indistinguishable from the same wine made from fresh fruit. As Morello cherries are somewhat hard to buy in their fresh state, the tinned variety is a great boon. A 6 lbs tin of fruit will make 2 gallons of wine, sweet or dry, but for a dessert wine use the 6 lbs tin for 1 gallon of wine.

Grape Concentrate
The winemakers' suppliers have a great range of grape concentrates which can be turned into a very palatable wine. These concentrates come from a variety of sources and vary greatly in quality. They all have more or less the same Specific Gravity but vary greatly in flavour and colour. Some of the red concentrates are degraded in colour and wines from these will be tawny in colour instead of the deep red desired. Some white concentrates are dark brown in colour and the wines from these are more golden white and lack the freshness aimed for. A useful addition to wines made from other bases is the addition of 1 pint (568 millilitres) of concentrate per gallon (5 litres) of wine.

All grape concentrates are heavily sulphited before canning, to preserve the contents and prevent the tins from blowing. This can make it difficult to get a must made from them to commence ferment-ing. To avoid this trouble all grape concentrates should be simmered (not boiled) in a saucepan, to drive off the sulphite before use. The normal additions to the must of yeast nutrient, vitamin B1 acid and tannin, must be used when making wines from the grape concentrates.

Giving your wine body

One of the failings in home-made wines is lack of vinosity or body. All wines that are sold commercially have this vinosity or body, to a greater or lesser degree due to the natural composition of the grape. To make up for this, home winemakers usually add certain extras to their recipes. The most common for red wines is raisins—which are, after all, only dried grapes. An addition of 1 lb (453 gms) per gallon of wine is the usual rate. Raisins are best added when making red wine of full flavour; if used in a white wine the addition of raisins would make the wine too dark in colour and the delicate flavour would be overlaid with the harsher flavour of the raisins.

An addition to white wines is 1 lb (453 gms) of sultanas which do not affect the colour or taste to the same degree. In both instances the raisins or sultanas should be minced before adding to the must. If you do not use a hydrometer it must be remembered that the addition of 1 lb of dried fruit, such as raisins or sultanas, will result in the addition of approximately 10 ozs (286 gms) of sugar to your must, and so that amount of cane sugar will not be needed. The amount of sugar in 1 lb of dried fruit will, of course, depend to a slight extent upon the quality of the fruit used.

Many winemakers these days are substituting 1 pint of red or white grape concentrate instead of raisins or sultanas. The only point to watch is the quality of the grape concentrate. Some of the concentrates of poorer quality will have a degrading effect in the colour of the wine. Some of the red grape concentrates are a reddish-brown instead of deep red and, as a result, the finished wine has a tendency towards a reddish-brown. Likewise, some of the white grape concentrates are slightly oxidised and instead of being light gold they are nearer to brown and, as a result, when added to a delicate pale wine, tend to darken it, so spoiling the wine. Where recipes include either dried fruit, such as raisins or sultanas or grape concentrate, then the amount of sugar that they contain has to be taken into account with the sugar addition stated.

Chapter 5
Racking, Clearing and Bottling

Racking

From the moment you pour your fermenting wine into your gallon jar, the wine commences to throw a deposit. The deposit consists of the lees of the yeast and small particles of the base material that has come through your straining cloth. If you squeezed the pulp very hard when straining, prior to pouring into the gallon jar, the build-up of deposit will be quite heavy and accumulate rather quickly. If this has happened then the wine should be racked. This is the removal of the wine from the heavy deposit at the bottom of the jar. The best way to accomplish this, is to lower the U-bend end of your syphon tube to just above the level of the deposit, having first stood your gallon jar upon a table. Now lower the other end of the syphon tube into a bucket on the floor. Suck air through the end of the tube in the bucket and as soon as the wine flows lower this end of the tube into the bucket. When the level of the wine in the gallon jar is level with the deposit in the gallon jar, stop the syphon and wash the deposit out of the gallon jar. Return the wine to the gallon jar and fill up the air space with sweetened water that has the same specific gravity of the wine that you have racked.

The wine will continue to ferment and throw a deposit, but the deposit that accumulates after the first racking will be much slower in build-up. Only if the deposit becomes heavy do you need to rack again before fermentation is completed. The best time to do this racking is when you intend to add more sugar to your wine but if you use this occasion to remove sediment, remember that the S.G. of the sugar water you add to take up the air space should be the same S.G. as your wine after you have made the sugar addition. Do not be worried if in the early stages your wine is very cloudy and opaque. You will find that as the fermentation progresses the wine will get clearer and the waste matter will form a sediment at the bottom of your container.

Clearing

Do not try to clear your wine with finings whilst it is fermenting. You will notice, during fermentation, streams of bubbles rising in your jar. This is the carbon dioxide gas which is formed when the yeast is converting the sugar into carbon dioxide gas and alcohol. These bubbles coming up with force from the bottom of your container are causing continual turbulence in the wine and causing small particles of the deposit to be continually mixed with the wine and, therefore, there is no point in trying to clear your wine whilst it is fermenting. Wait until fermentation is complete.

SYPHONING

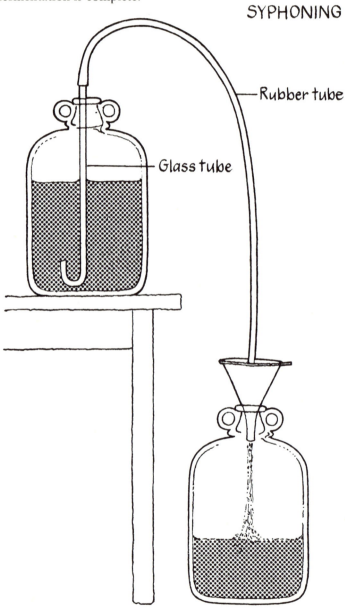

Rubber tube

Glass tube

The biggest difficulty that the newcomer to wine-making has is how to tell when the wine has completed its fermentation. If you are making a dry table wine and all your sugar has been added to your wine then fermentation is complete when your hydrometer shows a reading of below S.G. 00 and no bubbles are rising. When this position has been reached, put a rubber bung securely into the mouth of the gallon jar in place of the airlock and cork. Leave the wine for 12 hours. Then remove the rubber bung and listen to hear if there is any escape of gas. If there is, then the airlock and cork should be replaced and fermentation continued. If there is no escape of gas upon releasing the rubber bung, then replace it and leave the wine for 36 hours and again test. This can be repeated each time extending the time until the wine has been left bunged for a week. If after this length of time no gas escapes upon release of the rubber bung then you can rightly assume that fermentation has ceased.

With a sweet wine the time to test by use of the rubber bung is when the wine has consumed so much sugar that the yeast cannot work in the strength of alcohol produced. This is usually after about 3 lbs of sugar has been fermented although no hard and fast rule can be laid down. If the wine has consumed a large amount of sugar and the hydrometer still shows that the wine has some sweetness and no bubbles are rising, then use the rubber bung test as laid down for a dry wine. A point to remember is that the wine should be in a warm atmosphere before you check to see if the bubbles are still rising in your gallon jar. If the wine has been temporarily moved to a cold place this will slow—and in some instances stop—fermentation, and thus give a false impression that fermentation has indeed ceased.

There are several ways of clearing a wine once fermentation has ceased. Some wines when moved into a cold atmosphere for a couple of weeks will fall bright and clear without any further administrations. If this happens, well and good. Others may prove more stubborn. One of the most popular fining agents is called Bentonite. This is a form of clay, in powdered form, and can be obtained from wine equipment suppliers. Follow the instructions on the packet and add to the wine to be cleared. Stir well and leave for 7 days in a cool place and the wine should clear. Another popular fining agent is isinglass. This can also be obtained from suppliers. It is a milky white semi-glutinous fluid and is added at the rate of 2 teaspoonsful per gallon. The wine is again left in a cool place to clear. If all else fails you can resort to the use of asbestos pulp. To use this, get a large funnel about 8 ins in diameter and make a bed of cotton wool about 1 in deep in the mouth. Now take a piece of asbestos pulp about the size of an egg and mix with water until stirring it is the consistency of sloppy porridge. Pour this over the cotton wool, covering it completely. Allow to drain. Now gently pour the cloudy wine over the asbestos pulp breaking its fall with a saucer. After a few minutes the wine will flow through the funnel into your gallon jar. Again, after a few minutes, gently remove the funnel and remove the wine from the gallon jar; refilter this and then continue adding more wine to the funnel as the clear wine accumulates in the gallon jar. The success of this method depends on how well you make the bed of cotton wool. If you compress it too tightly the wine will be very slow coming through. If you do not press it tightly enough it will run through without clearing. It may take several attempts until you get the bed with the correct amount of compression.

There are many wine filter kits upon the market, the Harris Filter, Southern Vineyards, Vinbrite and Gey Owls kits are all very effective. But I feel that these are used to their best advantage to clear wines that have already been treated with either Bentonite or isinglass.

For those wishing to make up their own finings the following ingredients are needed: 1 oz (25 gms) isinglass, 2 drams (3 gms) citric acid, 3 drams ($4\frac{1}{2}$ gms) metabisulphite, 2 pints (approx 1 litre) cold water. Mix the above ingredients and stir well. Keep in a covered polythene bucket for about 3 days, by which time the acid will have cut the isinglass. Now stir well and pour into screw-topped bottles for use as required. The finings has a relatively short shelf-life and prolonged storage will reduce its efficiency.

Pectin Removal
Some wines even after all the usual attempts to clear them, remain stubbornly hazy. This may be due to what is known as a chemical haze and excessive treatment with finings will not clear them—in fact it may increase the haze. This is called a pectin haze and against such a haze normal fining is useless. To check a wine that you think has a pectin haze, take 2 teaspoonsful of wine in a glass, add 4 teaspoonsful of methylated spirits and mix well. Leave for a few minutes and then hold the glass of the mixture against a bright light. If small specks of jelly-like substance are in suspension in the liquid then the wine is suffering from pectin haze. The affected wine can be treated with pectin enzyme on sale at all suppliers and within a couple of weeks the wine will fall bright. The pectin haze can usually be eliminated from the wine by treating the must with pectin enzyme at the commencement of the winemaking. Fleshy fruits such as peaches, apples, plums, etc., are high in pectin content, as are parsnips and carrots. Avoid all

excessive boiling of this type of vegetable and so reduce the risk of pectin haze.

Polishing wines that have cleared
Sometimes after a wine has been successfully cleared it will throw a further sediment after storage and you will wish to make these wines star bright before bottling. Also, if you are putting wines into a show they may just lack that little bit of extra brightness. This can be easily achieved. You need cellulose pulp, a funnel and Whatman No 4 filter paper. The filter paper should be folded in half but do not press the crease right into the centre. Leave the centre half-inch uncreased. Now fold into quarters and eighths, remembering on each occasion not to carry the crease right into the centre. Open out and fit into the funnel. Add cellulose pulp at the rate of 1 teaspoonful to each bottle of wine to be filtered. This should make the wine thus filtered, star bright. The cellulose pulp does not leave any undesirable taste in the filtered wine.

Before attempting to bottle any wine you must ensure that the wine has finished fermenting and that it is perfectly clear. Never bottle in screw-topped bottles as this can be dangerous if the wine starts a secondary fermentation after bottling. Always use wine bottles and seal with a cork. Secondhand wine bottles are quite safe to use as long as they have been properly sterilised before use. Use a small 3 in. funnel and, if possible, buy one with an air vent in the stem. For home use, white wines can be bottled in any colour bottles but red wines should always be bottled in green- or brown-coloured bottles. When bottling for shows you must read the schedule carefully and bottle your exhibit in the style of bottle laid down for that particular competition. In all the large shows they usually stipulate punted Sauterne-type bottles of clear, colourless glass. This means exactly what it says, and bottles with a green tinge may lead to your exhibit being disqualified. The bottle should be filled within a quarter of an inch and three-quarters of an inch from the bottom of the stopper. For show purposes use all-cork stoppers. This is cork with a flange at the top. For home purposes you can either use all-cork stoppers or straight sided corks, but to use the latter a corking machine should be used. These are quite cheaply purchased. All corks must have an airtight fit. Stopper corks can be inserted by hand pressure; this will compress the air in the airspace between the wine and the bottom of the stopper and after a few minutes the cork stopper will ride upwards and in some case fly out of the bottle.

This can easily be avoided. Fill the bottle with wine to the correct height then take 18 ins of plastic covered wire, wrap one end around the hand, insert 2 ins of the other end of the wire into the bottle opening. Now press home the cork stopper until the stopper is right home. Pressing down on the top of the cork stopper, gently pull out the wire. The compressed air will follow the wire and the stopper cork will remain firmly in place.

Having successfully bottled your wine, label it—marking the type of wine, the style (sweet or dry) and the date made. Store the bottles in a cool, dry and dark place.

Chapter 6
Making a Typical Wine

Step-by-step guide

1. Crush fruit and place in container.

2. Add sufficient cold water to make quantity up to 6 pints.

3. Test acidity (by titration) and adjust acidity as required.

4. Add yeast nutrient, vitamin B1 additive and Campden tablets. Also Rohament P if required. Add pectic enzyme and tannin if required.

5. Take specific gravity and add sugar to give a starting gravity of 70 with a quantity of 1 gallon. Leave for 24 hours.

6. Add contents of yeast starter bottle (made 3 days prior to commencement of wine).

7. Stir regularly and ferment for 3 days.

8. Strain contents of container through straining bag.

9. Pour into gallon jar, insert airlock and cork.

10. Continue fermentation as near as possible to a temperature of 70°F (21°C).

11. As fermentation continues and sediment builds up in bottom of gallon jar, rack off sediment. Wash out gallon jar and return wine having checked Specific Gravity.

12. Fill up air space in top of gallon jar by adding sugar syrup of the same Specific Gravity as the wine.

13. Continue fermentation, checking S.G. from time to time.

14. When more sugar is required, rack off; add additional sugar and make up air space as before, if needed.

15. Continue fermentation until desired strength of alcohol and wine style (Sweet or Dry) has been obtained.

16. When fermentation has ceased, leave for 7 days to settle.

17. Now syphon off sediment and return wine to gallon jar. If in a hurry to bottle, add wine finings, clear and bottle. If gallon jar is not urgently required leave wine to ascertain if it will clear naturally and use finings as an ultimate resort to clear wine.

Popular myths dispelled

1. That windfalls or over-ripe or damaged fruit will make good wine. This is not true. The quality of a wine depends mainly upon the quality of the main base. Poor fruit never makes good wine.

2. That the longer a wine is matured, the stronger it becomes. I suppose everyone has heard the story of the person who was given a glass of 20-year-old Parsnip wine that was so strong that the one glass

made him drunk. The suggestion is that this was due to the wine's great age. Sad though it may be, the age of a wine has no bearing upon its alcoholic strength. This is determined by the amount of sugar that the yeast converted into alcohol during the making of the wine. Once the wine is made it will not get any stronger no matter how long it is kept.

3. That the greater the quantity of yeast put into the must, the greater will be the strength of the finished wine. This, again, is false. Extra yeast will only allow the wine to commence fermenting more quickly and will not have any relationship to the wine's strength. This is determined by the amount of sugar the yeast consumes.

4. That all wines have to be matured for many years to improve them. This is a common fallacy. Red wines usually need more maturing than white wines but no homemade wines need anything like the maturing time of commercial wines as they do not have the higher tannin content of commercial wines. The only reliable way to ascertain if your wine needs maturing is to taste it. If it is smooth and well balanced then drink it. If it is harsh or rough then mature it.

5. That wine can be made without yeast. Quite untrue. It is the action of the yeast converting the sugar into alcohol that is the heart of all wines.

6. That any wine made from grapes will be a good wine. This idea has caused many disappointments to winemakers. Commercial wine is made from wine grapes which are quite different from dessert grapes in the same way that cooking apples are different from eating apples. Very few dessert grapes can be made into a good quality wine.

7. The most popular myth is that the expert winemakers have special secret recipes that they do not divulge and that these are the reasons for their success.

The secret of success is not secret recipes but cleanliness, the best quality ingredients, a sound technique and a well-balanced recipe.

Faults and how to cure them
Acetification
This is caused by the vinegar bacillus, acetobar, which is around in the atmosphere. Once your wine is vinegary it is beyond help, so throw it away. Do not be dismayed. If you use Campden tablets with fresh fruit and do not over-expose your must or wine to the air this trouble is easily avoided.

Above left: Large fermentation container, with sieve for straining

Above right: Fermenting beer, showing 'rocky head' with top fermenting beer yeast

Below: Three gallon pan, wooden spoon and thermometer

 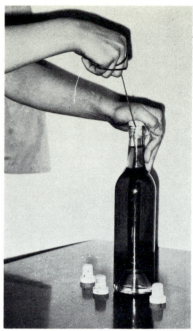

Above left: Corking. Inserting the cork with the aid of plastic wire to ensure that the cork remains seated

Above right: Corking. With the cork now firmly seated the wire is being withdrawn

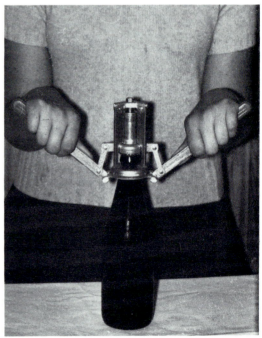

Right: The 'Crown Corker' in operation

Over-acid wines and under-acid wines
If you make a wine that is over-acid, the acidity can be reduced by use of pot. carbonate. As this can leave an unpleasant flavour the best way to deal with the wine is to blend the over-acid wine with a low acid wine. If you use an Acid Testing kit to test the acidity you should not have this trouble. Too little acid can be detected by a medicinal flat flavour in the finished wine. The addition of acid even at this late stage will improve the wine.

Wines lacking 'bite'
This is usually due to lack of tannin and is often more apparent in white wines. Tannin can be added even when the wine is made to correct this fault.

Clearing hazy wines
Test for pectin haze: 1 teaspoonful of wine to 4 of methylated spirits. If coagulations are observed treat with pectin enzyme to clear. Remember that the enzyme in liquid form has a limited shelf life. If no pectin is present, use wine finings and if this does not solve the problem, use betonite.

Crystals on bottom of bottle of wine
This worries some people but it is harmless. It is cream of tartar and, apart from the fact that the wine will be a little less acid when this happens, it in no way harms the wine.

Filtering
There are many very good filter kits on the market, such as Grey Owl, the Harris filter and the Vinbrite. Use of these will bring the desired clarity as long as the wine does not have a pectin haze.

Flowers of wine
This is a white powdery deposit on the top of the wine. It is a spoilage yeast and the wine will have a flat, watery taste, due to over-exposure to air and low alcohol level. It is not worth trying to cure, it is better to avoid it by keeping exposure to air to a minimum.

Mousiness
This is a very nasty after-taste in the wine, and the real cause is not known although lactic acid bacteria is suspected. It is not always apparent in the bouquet and sometimes the nasty after-taste is delayed for several seconds. The unusual aspect is that not everyone can

notice it. Some people will drink and enjoy a mousy wine whereas the same wine will be abhorrent to others. No cure, but it sometimes disappears. This is, without a doubt, the most baffling disease known to winemakers.

Off-flavours

These are often caused by leaving a wine or must to stand too long upon the lees (sediment). Rack off regularly, always making the quantity up by adding sugar water of the same S.G. as the racked wine.

Bitterness in a wine from citrus fruit is caused by the pith from the peel being added to the must. No cure, but the trouble can be avoided by making sure that when peel is used in a recipe no pith adheres to the peel.

Sticking fermentation

There are several causes: Too low a temperature or too high so that the yeast has been killed. When too low, move to a higher temperature. If too high, move to a cooler place and add another yeast starter.

Lack of nutrient: This should never occur as nutrients should be added to every must.

Lack of sugar: Check with hydrometer to ensure that sugar is present.

If a must or wine sticks and the yeast has not used up all the sugar present, make a fresh starter bottle and when it is working put it into a gallon jar. Now add a pint of the stuck wine and leave for a couple of days, when it should start fermenting. Repeat this process, adding the stuck wine by degrees until the whole wine is fermenting.

If in doubt about a wine, keep it and see if it changes with maturation.

Do not mistake acidity for dryness and *vice-versa*.

The secret to successful winemaking is to keep it clean, keep it simple and avoid gimmicks.

Chapter 7
Wine Competitions

Having made your wines and tried them on your friends, and I hope received their approval, you will still have doubts. Friends can sometimes let you down lightly when passing judgment upon your wines. The only way to obtain an unbiased opinion is to enter a wine competition. These competitions range from the small club show, through larger shows at the larger flower shows, on to regional home-wine-making shows to the ultimate in showing at the annual show of the National Association of Amateur Winemakers.

Wherever you show there are a number of cardinal rules that must be observed. First of all read carefully the show schedule and the rules governing the particular show in which you wish to exhibit your wines. Read carefully the way each class of wine is described, and pay special attention to the type of bottle admissible and where the label should be placed. In the smaller shows the details regarding bottles and labels may be rather sparse. The regional and national shows have more uniformity. The bottles are usually Sauterne-type with punted bottoms. The punt can be deep or shallow. The glass is usually described as clear white flint glass with rounded, not sloping, shoulders. Bottles with a green tinge are not acceptable.

The bottles should be filled so that when all the cork stopper is pushed home, the airspace between the bottom of the cork and the wine should be between one-quarter and three-quarters of an inch (6 mm to 19 mm approx).

Even if the rules of the particular show do not require this style of bottle it is better to get used to bottling this way and then, when you enter a large show, there is no danger of being disqualified due to the wrong type of bottle. Make sure that you get your entry to the show secretary in time and make a note of the closing time for entries to be staged at the show.

If you seriously intend to win prizes at shows, the best way to go about it is to read the previous schedules of the shows you intend to enter and then make your wines for this specific purpose. This is far better than looking at the schedule and trying to fit the wines you have made into the wines stipulated in the schedule.

We now come to the job of selecting wines for the particular show you have entered. If the schedule specifies 'Dry Wine' this is what it really means, and wines in this class should have an S.G. of 1·000 or below. The Sweet and Dessert wines should be sweet, but not to the extent that the sugar overrides the flavour and smothers it.

The real secret to a good wine is balance. This means a balance between flavour, bouquet, acidity and tannin content. The wine should be perfectly clear, with a good colour. 'Star bright' is the best way to describe the clarity. The wine when bottled should not have any minute particles suspended in it. Such particles are referred to by judges as 'floaters'. The best way to avoid floaters is to store your star bright wines in full gallon jars and when you syphon wine for a show from such jars only lower the U-bend of your syphon tube into the top half of the gallon jar and draw off sufficient for one and half bottles.

Having drawn off the wines you have available for a particular class, evaluate them one against the others for colour and clarity, bouquet, initial taste and after-taste (this is the taste in the mouth that lingers after the wine has been ejected). From this test you can then decide upon the wine you think is your best for that particular class. Repeat this for all the classes you have entered and then bottle them up as I have described. This should be done about two weeks prior to the show to give the wine time to settle down.

If you are fortunate to win a class, do not think that it will necessarily win the next time you show another bottle of the same wine. Remember that at the next show you may be up against a superior wine from another exhibitor. At the larger shows they often have a session during the afternoon called 'Judges at the Bar'. During this you can speak to the judge of the classes you entered and he will discuss with you the wine's qualities or defects. Having listened to these, when you have returned from the show re-taste your wines and see if you can match up with the judge's remarks your re-evaluation of your wine. But bear in mind that, although the general standard of judges is high, you can from time to time come upon one with slightly unusual ideas. But, win or lose, always accept the judge's rulings with good grace and try to do better next time.

A great help in appreciating what is a good table wine or a good dessert wine is to drink the equivalent style of commercial wine and get to understand the way these wines are balanced. However do not expect to reproduce their distinctive flavours as this is not possible. Showing is great fun, and it is the best way of getting an independent opinion of the quality of your wines. Don't be discouraged if you do not gain an award right away, and if you are successful, do not let success go to your head. It is so easy to win many prizes at one show and then, the next show you enter, not to win any award.

Chapter 8
Wine Recipes

The following recipes have all been made and found to be successful, making good quality wines. For the table wines the specific gravity given should not be varied by more than 5° up or down on the stated figure. Many winemakers may just wish to make dry wines, but not especially as table wines, to be drunk with a meal. These dry wines may be made to a much higher strength and the starting gravity stated for table wine can be ignored. If the wines are made stronger by the addition of more sugar, a slight increase in the base material should be made. Be careful not to add too much sugar in case you add more than the yeast can cope with and then it will be impossible to make the wine dry. To avoid this happening, add the additional sugar in small quantities, e.g. 4 ozs (114 gms) at a time, and do not add further sugar until the yeast has consumed each addition.

Sweet wine should only contain the degree of residual sugar that balances with the flavour and suits the individual palate of the winemaker. Some winemakers find a wine that has a finished gravity of 10 to be sweet enough for them to be a sweet wine, whilst other winemakers would need a finished gravity of as high as 20 for them to class it as a sweet wine.

Dessert wines should be full-bodied with a round, pronounced flavour, with a sugar balance to match the strength of flavour. The main failure in sweet and dessert wines is that there is often too much sweetness for the amount of flavour and then only the sugar predominates on the palate, killing the flavour completely.

Where acid is stated in a recipe this is only a general guide line. To obtain the best results the acidity of the must should be determined by use of a titration kit and adjusted accordingly, as the acid content of fruit varies from season to season.

All the recipes have been tried and proven but once the winemaker has confidence in his or her ability there is no reason why they cannot make their own variations of the recipes given. The only thing is that the overall balance of the wine in respect of acidity, tannin, body and amount of alcohol should be maintained. Until you have exhausted all the main wine bases do not waste time on gimmicky bases as they are seldom successful. In fact, beginners usually make every variety of wine for which they can obtain the necessary base and then, after a few years, decide that 5 or 6 bases are more to their liking than all the others and they then concentrate on making large quantities of a few wines.

Bouquet

Compared with the wines you buy, the homemade variety often fails to match up to them in the question of bouquet. With some homemade wines the bouquet from the fruit is strong enough to come through into the wine, but in others it is sometimes lacking, particularly in the case of red wines. This can, to a great extent, be overcome by the judicious use of rose petals. The addition of 2 flower heads of a strongly scented red rose to the must will usually be sufficient to give the wine a delicate bouquet without dominating it in bouquet or taste. I suggest that you use the flowers from either 'Wendy Cussons', 'Fragrant Cloud', 'Alec's Red' or 'Ernest H. Morse'. These roses have a strong bouquet and are ideally suited to this purpose. They are also the variety of rose that I would recommend to make a Rose Petal wine but, in this case, instead of 2 flower heads you would need sufficient petals to fill a quart jug ($9\frac{1}{2}$ litres) approx when gently pressed down.

For white wines, bouquet is a more difficult problem. Gooseberries for instance do not need any additions to give bouquet, whereas Parsley wine is improved by adding the thinly peeled rind of a lemon (no pith) to the must. There is great room for experiment in this field. The petals from 1 flower head of delicately scented elderflowers will often improve the bouquet of a white wine, giving it a hint of musk. But do not overdo the quantity of petals or else the flavour and taste of the wine will be dominated by the addition.

To sum up, my own approach to winemaking—aim for a balanced wine and if making a sweet wine make sure that the wine has sufficient flavour to match the residual sweetness. Always use the best quality of ingredients it is possible to obtain. Remember, if there is little or no flavour in a wine base before you turn it into wine, there will be no flavour in the resultant wine. I am of the opinion that the best wines are made from fruits. Carrots and parsnips are the only vegetable wines I think are worth making, and barley wine the only grain wine worthy of the trouble. Flower wines can be very good as long as the flowers used have a good bouquet but, here again, it is dangerous to be dogmatic about winemaking and from time to time I have drunk excellent wines made from the most bizarre bases. But I think that these are the exceptions rather than the rule. Winemaking is more of an art than a science. Cleanliness and attention to detail will ensure that you never make a bad wine, and occasionally produce a superb wine.

THE RECIPES

Red Table Wine (Dry)

Sloe Wine
4 lbs (2 kgs) ripe sloes
½ pt (284 ml) red grape concentrate
Yeast nutrient
2 Campden tablets
2 lbs (907 gms) sugar
Water to make up to 1 gallon (4½ litres)
Pure wine yeast starter

Method: Wash sloes, place in polythene bucket and crush by hand. Add grape concentrate and yeast nutrient. Add Campden tablets and leave covered for 36 hours. Now add sugar, stirring until dissolved. Add water to make up to 1 gallon. Add yeast starter and ferment on pulp for 3 days. Strain through straining bag and take reading of Specific Gravity. Add sugar syrup of same gravity to make up to 1 gallon of must. Ferment on in gallon jar fitted with airlock. Ferment to dryness. Clear and bottle.

Morello Cherry
4 lbs (2 kgs) ripe Morello cherries
Pectin enzyme
¼ teaspoonful tannin
2 Campden tablets
2 lbs (907 gms) sugar
Water to make 1 gallon (4½ litres)
Pure Wine yeast starter

Method: As for Sloe Wine, adding tannin at outset.

Bilberry Wine
¾ lb (341 gms) dried bilberries
Pectin enzyme
Yeast nutrient
1 teaspoonful citric acid
½ lb (226 gms) minced raisins
Sugar to give starting gravity 1·090
Water to make up to 1 gallon at above Specific Gravity
Pure wine yeast starter

Method: Wash bilberries and then boil for 10 minutes in ½ gallon of water. Pour the whole into polythene bucket, add minced raisins, citric acid and pectin enzyme. When cold, add water and sugar to make 1 gallon of must with a specific gravity of 90. Add yeast starter and ferment on pulp for 3 days. Strain through straining bag. Take Specific Gravity and add sugar syrup of the same gravity to make quantity up to 1 gallon. Ferment to dryness in gallon jar fitted with airlock. Clear and bottle.

Elderberry Wine
8 ozs (226 gms) dried elderberries
Pectin enzyme
Yeast nutrient
1 teaspoonful citric acid
½ lb (226 gms) minced raisins
Sugar to give starting gravity 90
Water to make up to 1 gallon
Pure wine yeast starter
    Method: As for Bilberry wine.

Cultivated Blackberry Wine
4 lbs (2 kgs) ripe cultivated blackberries
Pectin enzyme
2 Campden tablets
Yeast nutrient
Sugar to make starting gravity 90
Water to make 1 gallon
Pure wine yeast starter
    Method: Stand blackberries in cold water and remove any unripe berries or insects. Strain off water. Crush by hand and add pectin enzyme, yeast nutrient and Campden tablets. Leave covered for 24 hours. Now add water and sugar, after stirring, to give starting gravity 90. Add yeast starter and ferment on pulp for 3 days.
    Strain through straining bag. Take S.G. Add sugar syrup of same S.G. of must to make up to 1 gallon. Ferment to dryness in gallon jar with airlock. Clear and bottle.

Damson and Sloe Wine
2 lbs (907 gms) sloes, ripe
2 lbs (907 gms) damsons
Pectin enzyme
Yeast nutrient
2 Campden tablets
Water to make 1 gallon
Sugar to give starting gravity 90
Pure wine yeast starter

Method: Crush damsons and sloes by hand, add Campden tablets, yeast nutrient, pectin enzyme and ½ gallon cold water. Leave covered for 24 hours. Now add further water and sugar to make up to 1 gallon with gravity 90. Add yeast starter. Ferment on pulp for 2 days. Strain through straining bag. Take Specific Gravity and add sugar syrup of same gravity to make quantity up to 1 gallon. Ferment to dryness in gallon jar fitted with airlock. Clear and bottle.

White Table Wine (Dry)

Apple Wine
12 lbs (5½ kgs) apples
Rohament P
Yeast nutrient
Pectin enzyme
½ teaspoonful tannin
Water to make up to 1 gallon
2 Campden tablets
Sugar to give S.G. 90
Pure wine yeast starter

Method: Pour ½ gallon (2½ litres) of water into a polythene bucket and add two Campden tablets. Cut up the apples small, putting them into the water as you cut them up. Now add Rohament P and pectin enzyme and leave covered for 24 hours. Add tannin and sugar and water to make the quantity up to 1 gallon at 90 S.G. Stir in yeast starter and ferment on the must for 2 days. Strain through straining bag. Take Specific Gravity of must and add sufficient sugar water of the same gravity to bring total quantity up to 1 gallon. Put in gallon jar with airlock and ferment to dryness. Clear and bottle.

Apricot Wine
5½ lbs (2½ kgs) fresh apricots
1 teaspoon citric acid
Yeast nutrient
Rohament P
Pectin enzyme
½ teaspoonful tannin
2 Campden tablets
Water to make up to 1 gallon
Sugar to give starting gravity of 90

Method: Cut apricots in half and remove stones. Place apricots in bucket and crush by hand. Add tannin, Rohament P, pectin enzyme acid and yeast nutrient. Add water to make up to ½ gallon. Cover and leave for 24 hours. Add sugar and water to make quantity up to 1 gallon with Specific Gravity 90. Stir in yeast starter and ferment on pulp for 3 days. Strain and pour into gallon jar, making quantity up to 1 gallon with sugar syrup of the same gravity as the strained must. Fit airlock and ferment to dryness. Clear and bottle.

Peach Wine
6 lbs fresh peaches (2½ kgs) approx
Yeast nutrient
Pectin enzyme
Rohament P
1 teaspoonful citric acid
½ teaspoonful tannin
Water to make 1 gallon
Sugar to give starting gravity 90
Yeast starter
   Method: Cut the peaches in half and remove stones. Then cut out the discoloured area where stone has been. Crush the cut-up fruit and put in bucket. Add tannin, pectin enzyme, Rohament P and citric acid. Crush and add Campden tablets and leave covered for 24 hours. Then add water and sugar to make up to 1 gallon with Specific Gravity of 90. Stir in yeast starter and ferment on pulp for 3 days. Strain and add sugar syrup of same gravity of strained must to make quantity up to 1 gallon. Pour into gallon jar. Insert airlock and ferment to dryness. Clear and bottle.

Fresh Parsley Wine
6 ozs (171 gms) fresh parsley
Juice 1 lemon
½ teaspoonful tannin
Yeast nutrient
Thinly peeled rind of 1 lemon (*no* pith)
½ lb (227 gms) minced sultanas or ½ pint (¼ litre) grape concentrate
   (white)
Sugar to give starting gravity 90
Water to make up to 1 gallon
Pure wine yeast starter
   Method: Boil the fresh parsley in 1 quart of water for 20 minutes. Strain boiled water into polythene bucket. Throw away parsley. Into the bucket place sultanas or grape concentrate and add lemon juice, lemon peel, tannin, yeast nutrient, and stir. Leave covered for 24 hours. Take Specific Gravity of the must and add water and sugar to

make up to 1 gallon with an S.G. of 90. Now stir in yeast starter. Ferment on the pulp for 3 days then strain off into gallon jar, adding sugar and water to make quantity up to 1 gallon at the same Specific Gravity as the must after straining. Insert airlock and ferment to dryness. Clear and bottle.

Gooseberry Wine
2¼ lbs (1 kg) dessert gooseberries (e.g. Leveller or Careless variety dessert gooseberries)
1 lb (454 gms) green gooseberries
1 lb (454 gms) minced sultanas
Pectin enzyme
Rohament P
2 Campden tablets
Yeast nutrient
Sugar to give starting gravity of 90
Water to make up to 1 gallon
Pure wine yeast starter
    Method: Put gooseberries into polythene bucket. Pour over them 1 quart of boiling water. When cold, crush gooseberries by hand and add Campden tablets, pectin enzyme, Rohament P., minced sultanas and yeast nutrient, and leave covered for 24 hours. Then stir well. Take S.G. and add sugar and water to make up to 1 gallon with an S.G. 90. Add yeast starter and ferment on pulp for 3 days. Strain and put into gallon jar, adding sugar syrup of the same S.G. as the strained must to make quantity up to 1 gallon. Ferment to dryness. Clear and bottle.

Grape Foliage Wine
6½ lbs (3 kgs) grape leaves and prunings (taken at first pruning)
1 lb (454 gms) minced sultanas
1 teaspoonful citric acid
½ teaspoonful tannin
Pectin enzyme
Rohament P
2 Campden tablets
Yeast nutrient
Sugar to give starting gravity 95
Water to make up to 1 gallon
Yeast starter
    Method: Cut up the grape foliage small and place in bucket. Pour over 1 quart (1¼ litres) boiling water and add minced sultanas, tannin,

pectin enzyme, Rohament P and citric acid and leave to go cold. Then add 2 Campden tablets and cover. Leave for 24 hours, then add sugar and water to make up to 1 gallon at S.G. 95. Stir in yeast starter and ferment on pulp for 2 days. Strain. Take S.G. reading. Add sugar syrup of the same S.G. to make quantity up to 1 gallon. Pour into gallon jar, insert airlock and ferment to dryness. Clear and bottle.

Red Wine (Sweet)
Morello Cherry
6½ lbs (3 kgs) Morello cherries
½ teaspoonful tannin
Yeast nutrient
Pectin enzyme
2 Campden tablets
Sugar to make sweet wine
Water to make 1 gallon
Pure wine yeast starter

Method: Wash cherries and put into polythene bucket. Crush by hand and add yeast nutrient, tannin and pectin enzyme. Add 2 Campden tablets and leave covered for 24 hours. Add sugar and water to make 1 gallon at S.G. 70. Stir in yeast starter and ferment on pulp for 3 days. Strain off, take S.G. and then add sugar syrup of the same S.G. as the strained must to make up to 1 gallon. Pour into gallon jar, insert airlock and ferment on. When dry, add sugar to bring S.G. from 0 to 40 and ferment on. When fermented to dryness again add sugar to bring S.G. from 0 to desired finished gravity for a sweet wine. Ferment on until dryness and repeat sugar additions until wine stops fermenting with sugar still present. Then add sugar to bring to desired sweetness. Clear and bottle.

Special Note concerning addition of sugar
It may take more than 2 additions of sugar to reach the stage where the yeast has reached its alcohol tolerance with sugar still present in the wine.

To explain the sugar addition in detail (as this will apply to all sweet wines) I give the following example:

1. Initial addition of sugar at must stage brings S.G. to 70. Ferment to dryness (0).

2. Add sugar to raise S.G. from 0 to 40. Ferment to dryness.

From this stage you decide at what S.G. you want the finished wine to be. If you desire a finished wine with a gravity of 15 then, at stage 3, you add sugar to bring S.G. to 15. Ferment to dryness and keep repeating this process until wine stops fermenting with sugar still present in the wine. You then add sufficient sugar to bring the wine to a S.G. of 15. Clear and bottle.

If you wish for a wine with a finished S.G. of 10 then at stage 3 you will add sugar to give a S.G. of 10, fermenting to dryness and repeating the addition until yeast stops with sugar present and then add sufficient sugar to raise final S.G. to 10 again. Clear and bottle.

Raspberry Sweet
4½ lbs (3 kgs) raspberries
Yeast nutrient
Vitamin B1
½ teaspoonful tannin
Pectin enzyme
2 Campden tablets
Water to make 1 gallon
Sugar as required for sweet wine
Pure wine yeast starter
  Method: Place raspberries in bucket and crush by hand. Add tannin, yeast nutrient, vitamin B1 tablet (3 mg), pectin enzyme and 2 Campden tablets. Cover and leave for 24 hours. Then add water and sugar to give starting gravity of 70. Add yeast starter and ferment on pulp for 3 days. Strain off, add sugar syrup—same S.G. as strained must—to make up to 1 gallon. Pour into gallon jar, insert airlock and ferment on to dryness. Add sugar as suggested for sweet Morello wine. Clear and bottle.

Damson—Sweet
4½ lbs (2 kgs) damsons
Yeast nutrient
Vitamin B1 (3 mg) tablets
Pectin enzyme
Rohament P
2 Campden tablets
Water to make up to 1 gallon
Sugar as for sweet wine
Pure wine yeast starter
  Method: Wash damsons and place in bucket. Crush by hand, adding yeast nutrient, Vitamin B1 tablets, pectin enzyme, Rohament P and 2 Campden tablets. Pour over 1 quart (1¼ litres) approx, of cold water. Cover and leave for 24 hours. Add sugar and water to make up to 1 gallon at S.G. 70. Stir in yeast starter and ferment on pulp for 3

days. Strain and take S.G. Add sugar syrup of the same S.G. as the strained must to make up to 1 gallon. Pour into gallon jar and insert airlock. Ferment on, adding sugar as per sweet Morello Cherry recipe. Clear and bottle.

Elderberry Sweet
3¼ lbs (1½ kgs) of strigged elderberries
2 rose heads of red scented rose petals (e.g. 'Wendy Cussons')
Pectin enzyme
Yeast nutrient
Vitamin B1 tablets
1 teaspoonful citric acid
½ lb (227 gms) minced raisins
2 Campden tablets
Sugar as required for sweet wine
Water to make up to 1 gallon
Pure wine yeast starter
Method; Boil the elderberries in 1 quart of water for 10 minutes. Then pour the contents of the saucepan into a polythene bucket. Add yeast nutrient, Vitamin B1 tablet, citric acid, pectin enzyme, rose petals, minced raisins. When liquid is cold, add Campden tablets and leave covered for 24 hours. Then add sugar and water to make up to 1 gallon with S.G. of 70. Stir in yeast starter and ferment on pulp for 3 days. Then strain. Take S.G. of strained must and add sugar syrup of the same S.G. to make up to 1 gallon. Pour into gallon jar, insert airlock. Ferment on, adding sugar as for sweet wine. Then clear and bottle.

Blackberry Wine
4½ lbs (2 kgs) wild blackberries
Yeast nutrient
Vitamin B1 tablet
Pectin enzyme
Sugar as for sweet wine
2 Campden tablets
Water to make up to 1 gallon
Pure wine yeast starter
Method; Clean blackberries. Put into bucket and crush by hand. Add yeast nutrient, Vitamin B1 tablet, pectin enzyme, 1 quart cold water and 2 Campden tablets. Cover and leave for 24 hours. Then add water and sugar to make up to 1 gallon with S.G. 70. Stir in yeast starter and ferment on pulp for 3 days. Strain and take S.G. Now add

sugar syrup of the same S.G. to make quantity up to 1 gallon. Pour into gallon jar and insert airlock. Ferment on, adding sugar as required for sweet wine (see Morello cherry). Clear and bottle.

White or Golden Wines (Sweet)
Gooseberry Wine—Sweet
4½ lbs (2 kgs) ripe dessert gooseberries
Yeast nutrient
Vitamin B1 tablet
½ teaspoonful tannin
2 Campden tablets
Pectin enzyme
Sugar as per sweet wine
Water to make up to 1 gallon
Pure wine yeast starter
   Method: As for Blackberry (Sweet).

Prune and Date Wine
2¼ lbs (1 kg) prunes
1 lb (453 gms) dates
1 teaspoonful citric acid
Yeast nutrient and Vitamin B1 tablet
½ teaspoonful tannin
Pectin enzyme
Rohament P
Sugar as for sweet wine
Water to make up to 1 gallon
Pure wine yeast starter
   Method: Simmer prunes in 1 quart water for 30 minutes. Pour contents of saucepan into bucket. When cold, crush prunes. Add chopped dates, citric acid, tannin, yeast nutrient, Vitamin B1 tablet, pectin enzyme, Rohament P and add 1 quart cold water. When must is cold, add 2 Campden tablets and leave covered for 24 hours. Then add sugar and water to make 1 gallon at S.G. 70. Stir in yeast starter and ferment on pulp for 3 days. Strain, take S.G. and add sugar syrup of same S.G. to make quantity up to 1 gallon. Pour into gallon jar and insert airlock. Ferment on, adding sugar as required for sweet wine. Clear and bottle.

Golden Plum—Sweet
4½ lbs (2 kgs) ripe golden plums
Yeast nutrient

Vitamin B1 tablets
1 teaspoonful citric acid
½ teaspoonful tannin
Pectin enzyme
Rohament P
2 Campden tablets
Water to make 1 gallon
Sugar as required for sweet wine
Pure wine yeast starter

Method: Place plums into bucket and crush by hand. Add citric acid, yeast nutrient, Vitamin B1 tablets, tannin, pectin enzyme, Rohament P, 1 quart cold water and add 2 Campden tablets. Cover and leave for 24 hours. Add water and sugar to make 1 gallon at S.G. 70. Stir in yeast starter and ferment on pulp for 3 days. Strain and take S.G. of must. Add sugar syrup of same gravity to make up to 1 gallon. Pour into gallon jar, insert airlock. Ferment on, adding sugar as required for sweet wine. Clear and bottle.

Rose Hip and Fig Wine
½ lb dried rose hip shells
4 ozs (114 gms) figs
½ teaspoonful citric acid
Pectin enzyme
Rohament P
Yeast nutrient
Vitamin B1 tablet
Water to make up to 1 gallon
Sugar as required
Pure wine yeast starter

Method: Place dried rose hip shells into bucket, adding chopped-up figs, tannin, citric acid, pectin enzyme, Rohament P, yeast nutrient, and Vitamin B1 tablet. Pour over 6 pints (3½ litres) boiling water. When cold, add sugar and water to make up to 1 gallon with S.G. 70. Stir in yeast starter and ferment on pulp for 4 days. Strain and take S.G. of must. Add sugar syrup of same S.G. to make up to 1 gallon. Pour into gallon jar and insert airlock. Ferment on, adding sugar as required for sweet wine. Clear and bottle.

Red Dessert Wines
The main difference between the sweet wine recipes and dessert recipes is that the dessert recipes are made to a higher degree of sweetness, usually a finished gravity of from S.G. 15 and upwards

Two styles of punted Sauterne bottles accepted in major competitions

Wine bottles correctly filled ready for competition

Below: Show-style beer bottles with closures

A selection of crystal glasses. A good wine merits glasses such as these

Some of the cups and other awards won by the author for both wine and beermaking

Various styles of beer glasses

according to taste. They have a greater quantity of fruit per gallon of wine to balance up with this extra residual sugar. The method of feeding the wine with sugar to obtain the maximum alcohol content with high residual sugar is the same as outlined in the recipe for Morello wine sweet, but when the wine has finished fermenting more sugar is added to give the higher residual sugar S.G.

Bilberry Wine
4½ lbs (2 kgs) fresh bilberries
1 teaspoonful citric acid
Yeast nutrient
Vitamin B1 tablet (93 mg)
1 lb (453 gms) minced raisins
2 rose heads of red scented rose petals
Pectin enzyme
2 Campden tablets
Sugar for dessert wine
Water to make 1 gallon
Pure wine yeast starter

Method: Place bilberries in bucket and crush by hand. Add citric acid, yeast nutrient, Vitamin B1 tablet, minced raisins, rose petals and 1 quart of cold water. Add 2 Campden tablets and leave covered for 24 hours. Now add sugar and water to make 1 gallon at S.G. 70. Ferment on pulp for 3 days. Strain and take S.G. of must. Add sugar syrup of same S.G. to make up to 1 gallon. Pour into gallon jar, insert airlock and ferment on adding sugar as required for dessert wine. Clear and bottle.

Blackberry Dessert Wine
6½ lbs (3 kgs) wild blackberries
1 lb minced raisins
Yeast nutrient
Vitamin B1 tablet
Pectin enzyme
2 flower heads of scented red roses
½ teaspoonful citric acid
Water to make up to 1 gallon
Yeast starter
Sugar as for dessert wine

Method: Wash blackberries, put into bucket and crush by hand. Add minced raisins, rose petals, yeast nutrient, Vitamin B1, pectin enzyme and 2 Campden tablets. Now add 1¾ pints (1 litre) cold water.

Cover and leave for 24 hours. Now add water and sugar to give S.G. 70 and stir in yeast starter.

Ferment on pulp for 3 days. Strain and take S.G. Now make quantity up to 1 gallon by adding sugar syrup of the same S.G. Pour into gallon jar and ferment on, adding sugar as required for dessert wine. Clear and bottle.

Elderberry, Port-style
4½ lbs (2 kgs) elderberries (fresh, having been removed from stalks before weighing)
1 lb (454 gms) minced raisins
2 flower heads red scented roses
Pectin enzyme
1 teaspoonful citric acid
Yeast nutrient
Vitamin B1 tablet
2 Campden tablets
Water to make 1 gallon
Pure wine yeast starter

Method: Place elderberries in bucket and crush by hand (to avoid stained hands, wear rubber gloves). Now add raisins, flower petals, pectin enzyme, citric acid, yeast nutrient, Vitamin B1 and Campden tablets. Pour over 2¾ pints (1½ litres) cold water. Cover and leave for 24 hours. Now stir and add sugar and water to make up to 1 gallon with S.G. 70 approx. Stir in yeast starter and ferment on pulp for 3 days. Then strain, take S.G. and add sugar and water to make 1 gallon at same S.G. as after straining. Pour into gallon jar, insert airlock and ferment on, adding sugar as for dessert wine. Clear and bottle.

Damson Dessert Wine
6½ lbs (3 kgs) ripe damsons
½ pint (¼ litre) red grape concentrate
Pectin enzyme
Yeast nutrient
Vitamin B1 tablet
2 Campden tablets
Water to make up to 1 gallon
Sugar as for dessert wine
Pure wine yeast starter

Method: Wash damsons and place in bucket. Crush by hand. Add minced raisins, yeast nutrient, Vitamin B1, pectin enzyme, grape concentrate and Campden tablets. Pour over 2¾ pints (1½ litres) cold water. Leave covered for 24 hours. Now stir and add sugar and water to make up to 1 gallon at approx 70 S.G. Stir in yeast starter and ferment on pulp for 3 days. Strain and check S.G. Now add sugar syrup of same S.G. to make up to 1 gallon. Pour into gallon jar, inserting airlock. Ferment on, adding sugar as required for dessert wine. Clear and bottle.

Loganberry Wine
5½ lbs (2½ kgs) loganberries
1 lb (453 gms) minced raisins
Pectin enzyme
Yeast nutrient
Vitamin B1 tablet
2 Campden tablets
Water to make 1 gallon
Sugar as for dessert wine
Pure wine yeast starter
    Method: Wash loganberries and place in bucket. Crush by hand, add minced raisins, pectin enzyme, yeast nutrient, Vitamin B1 tablet, and Campden tablets. Pour over 2¾ pints (1½ litres) cold water. Cover and leave for 24 hours. Stir and add sugar and water to make 1 gallon at approx 70 S.G. Stir yeast starter and ferment on pulp for 3 days. Then strain and take S.G. Now add sugar syrup of same S.G. to make up to 1 gallon. Pour into gallon jar, insert airlock and ferment on, adding sugar as required for dessert. Clear and bottle.

Raspberry Dessert Wine
5½ lbs (2½ kgs) fresh raspberries
1 pint (½ litre) red grape concentrate
1 teaspoonful tannin
Yeast nutrient
Vitamin B1 tablets
2 Campden tablets
Pectin enzyme
Water to make 1 gallon
Sugar as required for dessert wine
Yeast starter
    Method: As for loganberry wine.

White or Golden Dessert Wines
Golden Plum Wine
6½ lbs ripe golden plums

½ pint (284 ml) white grape concentrate
Pectin enzyme
Rohament P
½ teaspoonful tannin
Yeast nutrient
Vitamin B1 tablet
2 Campden tablets
Water to make 1 gallon
Sugar as for dessert wine
Pure wine yeast starter

Method: Cut plums in half and remove stones. Place plums in bucket and crush by hand. Add grape concentrate, pectin enzyme, Rohament P, yeast nutrient, Vitamin B1 tablet, tannin and 2 Campden tablets. Pour over 2¾ pints (1½ litres) cold water. Cover and leave for 24 hours. Add sugar and water to make 1 gallon with S.G. approx 70. Stir in pure wine yeast starter and ferment on pulp for 3 days. Strain and take S.G. Add sugar syrup of same gravity to make up to 1 gallon. Pour into gallon jar, insert airlock and ferment on, adding sugar as required for a dessert wine. Clear and bottle.

Banana and Fig Wine
3¼ lbs (1½ kgs) peeled bananas
½ lb (226 gms) chopped figs
2 teaspoonsful citric acid
Pectin enzyme
Rohament P
1 teaspoonful tannin
2 Campden tablets
Yeast nutrient
Vitamin B1 tablet
Water to make 1 gallon
Sugar as for dessert wine
Pure wine yeast starter

Method: Place bananas and figs in bucket. Pour over 2¾ pints (1½ litres) boiling water. When cold, crush by hand and add citric acid, tannin, pectin enzyme, Rohament P, yeast nutrient, Vitamin B1 tablet and Campden tablets. Cover and leave 24 hours. Add sugar and water to make 1 gallon at about 70 S.G. Stir in wine yeast starter and ferment on pulp for 3 days. Now strain. Take S.G. of must and add sugar syrup of same gravity to make up to 1 gallon. Pour into gallon jar, insert airlock and ferment on, adding sugar as required for dessert wine. Clear and bottle.

Muscatel Raisin Wine
(This wine usually requires 2 years maturation)
4½ lbs (2 kgs) muscatel raisins
Yeast nutrient
Vitamin B1 tablet
1 teaspoonful citric acid
Pectin enzyme
Rohament P
Water to make 1 gallon
Sugar as for dessert wine
Pure wine yeast starter

Method: Mince the muscatel raisins and pour over 3½ pints boiling water (2 litres). Add yeast nutrient, Vitamin B1 tablet and citric acid, pectin enzyme, Rohament P. When cold, make up to 1 gallon by adding cold water and sugar to make S.G. approx 70. Stir in yeast starter. Ferment on pulp for 4 days. Strain. Take S.G. and add sugar syrup of same gravity to make quantity up to 1 gallon. Pour into gallon jar, insert airlock and ferment on, adding sugar as for dessert wine. Clear and bottle.

Date Wine
3¼ lbs (1½ kgs) dates
2 teaspoonsful citric acid
Yeast nutrient
Vitamin B1 tablet
Pectin enzyme
Rohament P
½ teaspoonful tannin
Water to make 1 gallon
Sugar as for dessert wine
Pure wine yeast starter

Method: Cut up dates and place in bucket. Pour over 3½ pints (2 litres) boiling water. Add citric acid, yeast nutrient, Vitamin B1 tablet, pectin enzyme, Rohament P and tannin. When cold, make up to 1 gallon by adding cold water and sugar to give S.G. approx 70. Stir in yeast starter and ferment on pulp for 3 days. Strain and take S.G. Make up to 1 gallon with sugar syrup of same S.G. Pour into gallon jar. Insert airlock and ferment on, adding sugar as required for dessert wine. Clear and bottle.

Gooseberry Dessert Wine
6½ lbs (3 kgs) ripe dessert gooseberries

$\frac{1}{2}$ pt (284 ml) white grape concentrate
Pectin enzyme
Rohament P
$\frac{1}{2}$ teaspoonful tannin
Yeast nutrient and Vitamin B1 tablet
Water to make 1 gallon
Sugar as for dessert wine
Pure wine yeast starter

Method: Place gooseberries in bucket and pour over $2\frac{3}{4}$ pints ($1\frac{1}{2}$ litres) boiling water. When cold, crush gooseberries by hand and add grape concentrate, pectin enzyme, Rohament P, tannin, yeast nutrient and Vitamin B1 tablet. Add sugar and water to make quantity up to 1 gallon with an S.G. of approx 70. Stir in yeast starter and ferment on pulp for 3 days. Strain and take S.G. Now add sugar syrup of same S.G. to make quantity up to 1 gallon. Pour into gallon jar. Insert airlock and ferment on, adding sugar as required for a dessert wine. Clear and bottle.

Citrus Wines
Orange Wine
6 sweet oranges (Valencia, if obtainable)
6 bitter oranges
1 lb (454 mgs) minced raisins
1 teaspoonful tannin
Yeast nutrient
Vitamin B1 tablet
Pectin enzyme
Water to make 1 gallon
Sugar to give starting gravity 90 for dry wine. Additional sugar for
    sweet wine
Pure wine yeast starter

Method: Peel the oranges thinly with sharp knife, avoiding any pith. Place the peel under the grill with a low light, to brown the peel. (Watch the peel carefully and turn it regularly until brown. Do not use a high heat as, when dry, peel catches alight quite easily. Place browned peel in bucket and pour over $2\frac{3}{4}$ pints ($1\frac{1}{2}$ litres) boiling water. Leave to cool. Now take the 12 peeled oranges and express the juice on lemon squeezer. Pour this juice into another bucket, adding raisins, tannin, yeast nutrient, Vitamin B1 tablet, pectin enzyme, and strain the water off the peel in the first bucket. Throw away peel and add the liquid to the second bucket. Add sugar and water to make 1 gallon with S.G. 90. Stir in wine yeast starter and ferment on pulp for 3 days. Strain.

Take S.G. and add sugar syrup of same S.G. to make up to 1 gallon. Pour into gallon jar. Insert airlock. Ferment to dryness for dry wine. Add additional sugar as required for sweet wine. Clear and bottle.

Tangerine Wine
12 tangerines or satsumas
Pectin enzyme
1 lb (454 gms) minced sultanas
½ teaspoonful tannin
Yeast nutrient
Vitamin B1 tablet
Water to make 1 gallon
Sugar for dry or sweet wine
Pure wine yeast starter
    Method: Peel tangerines thinly, avoiding any pith. Place peel in bucket. Express juice from peeled tangerines on lemon squeezer and add to bucket. Add raisins, pectin enzyme, tannin, yeast nutrient, Vitamin B1 tablet, sugar and water to make up to 1 gallon with S.G. 90. Ferment on pulp for 3 days, having added yeast starter. Then strain and take S.G. Add sugar syrup of same S.G. to make quantity up to 1 gallon. Pour into gallon jar, insert airlock and ferment to dryness for dry wine. Add sugar as required for sweet wine.

Grapefruit Wine
6 large grapefruit (West Indian or Nigerian, if at all possible)
1 pint (½ litre) white grape concentrate
Pectin enzyme
½ teaspoonful tannin
Yeast nutrient
Vitamin B1 tablet
Sugar to give starting S.G. 90
Water to make 1 gallon
Pure wine yeast starter
    Method: Cut the grapefruit in half and express juice on a lemon squeezer and pour into bucket. Add raisins, pectin enzyme, tannin, yeast nutrient, Vitamin B1 tablet and water and sugar to make 1 gallon with S.G. 90. Stir in wine yeast starter. Ferment on pulp for 3 days. Strain. Take S.G. and add sugar syrup of same S.G. to make up to 1 gallon. Pour into gallon jar. Insert airlock. Ferment to dryness. Clear and bottle.
    For sweet wine, make additions of sugar, as suggested, in Sweet Morello Cherry recipe.

Vegetable Wines
Although many winemakers find vegetables a good base from which to make wines I would personally recommend only two: parsnips and carrots. Vegetables have to be boiled in water and the water used as the main base. A word of warning—do not over boil and be sure to cut the vegetables into (as far as possible) equally sized pieces. Boil the vegetables until they can just be pierced with a fork. It is better to under boil than to over boil. Over boiling will cause excessive pectin haze.

Parsnip Wine
6½ lbs (3 kgs) parsnips
1 lb minced sultanas or raisins
1 teaspoonful citric acid
½ teaspoonful tannin
Yeast nutrient
Vitamin B1 tablet
Water to make 1 gallon
Sugar for dry or sweet wines as desired
Pure wine yeast starter
    Method: Wash parsnips and cut up into equally sized pieces. Place in saucepan and cover with water. Boil gently until parsnips can be pierced with a fork. Strain the water from the parsnips and throw parsnips away. Place the boiled parsnip water into a bucket and add raisins/sultanas, citric acid, tannin, yeast nutrient and Vitamin B1 tablet. Add sufficient sugar and cold water to make quantity up to 1 gallon with an S.G. of 90. Ferment on pulp for 3 days. Now strain and take S.G. adding sugar syrup of the same gravity to make quantity up to 1 gallon.
    Pour into gallon jar, insert airlock and ferment to dryness for dry wine. Add further sugar if sweet wine is required. Clear and bottle.

Carrot Wine
6¾ lbs (3 kgs) washed carrots
1 lb minced sultanas
1 teaspoonful citric acid
½ teaspoonful tannin
Yeast nutrient
Vitamin B1 tablet
Water to make 1 gallon
Sugar for style of wine desired
Pure wine yeast starter.
    Method: As for parsnip wine.

Dried Herb Wines

There are various herb wines or dried flower wines that can be made, such as parsley, lemon thyme, dandelion, etc. The following is a basic recipe which can be adopted for any dried herbs or dried flower petal wine.

Herb or Dried Flower Petal Wine
2 ozs (57 gms approx) of dried herbs or flower petals
1 lb (454 gms) minced sultanas
1 teaspoonful citric acid
1 teaspoonful tannin
Yeast nutrient
Vitamin B1 tablet
Sugar for dry or sweet wine
Water to make up to 1 gallon
Pure wine yeast starter

Method: Place herbs or petals in saucepan and pour over $2\frac{3}{4}$ pints ($1\frac{1}{2}$ litres) of water. Bring to boil and simmer for 20 minutes. Now pour contents of saucepan into bucket. Add sultanas, citric acid, tannin, yeast nutrient, Vitamin B1 tablet. Now add sufficient water and sugar to make up to 1 gallon with a S.G. 90 (take S.G. when liquid is cold). Now stir in yeast starter and ferment on pulp for 3 days. Strain. Take S.G. and add sugar syrup of same gravity to make up to 1 gallon. Insert airlock and ferment to dryness for dry wine. Add further sugar as required for sweet wine. Clear and bottle.

Flower Wines

Flowers can be turned into a pleasant wine but it must be remembered that all you get from the flowers is the bouquet, which in turn gives the wine its flavour. You must therefore only make wine from flowers with a strong and pleasant scent. The two most popular are Rose Petal and Elderflower. For rose petal wine, red roses with a strong scent are required such as 'Fragrant Cloud', 'Wendy Cussons' or similar roses.

The elderflowers are more difficult to use as so many elderflowers have a strong pungent smell, similar to that left by tom cats—hence it is called 'catty' by winemakers. If you search around you will find some bushes with flowers that have a delicate musky scent and these are the ones to use. Note where the bush is for future reference. Flowers having a sweet scent give an impression of sweetness to the wine and less residual sugar is required to give a sweet finish.

Rose Petal

Sufficient scented red rose petals to fill a quart (approx 1 litre) jug
  when gently pressed down
1 teaspoonful tannin
1 teaspoonful citric acid
$\frac{1}{2}$ pint (284 ml) red grape concentrate
Yeast nutrient
Vitamin B1 tablet
Sugar for dry wine—starting S.G. 90
Water to make up to 1 gallon

Method: Place rose petals in bucket and pour over $2\frac{3}{4}$ pints ($1\frac{2}{3}$ litres) boiling water. Add all other ingredients except yeast starter. Make quantity up to 1 gallon with S.G. 90. When cold, stir in yeast starter. Ferment on pulp for 3 days. Strain. Take S.G. and add sugar syrup of same gravity to make up to 1 gallon. Pour into gallon jar, insert airlock and ferment to dryness for dry wine. Add further sugar for sweet wine but finish with a lower residual sugar than you would usually have for a sweet wine. Clear and bottle.

Elderflower Wine

1 pint (568 ml) elderflower petals (sufficient to fill 1 quart—approx
  1 litre jug) after being gently pressed down
$\frac{1}{2}$ lb (226 gms) minced sultanas
1 teaspoonful citric acid
1 teaspoonful tannin
Yeast nutrient
Vitamin B1 tablet
2 Campden tablets
Sugar for dry wine
Water to make 1 gallon
Pure wine yeast starter

Method: Place elderflowers in bucket and pour over $2\frac{3}{4}$ pints ($1\frac{1}{2}$ litres) cold water. Add sultanas, citric acid, tannin, yeast nutrient, Vitamin B1 tablet and 2 Campden tablets. Cover and leave for 24 hours. Then add sugar and water to make up to 1 gallon with a gravity of 90. Stir in yeast starter and ferment on pulp for 3 days. Strain. Take S.G. and add sugar syrup of same gravity to make quantity up to 1 gallon. Pour into gallon jar, insert airlock and ferment on to dryness. Clear and bottle.

This wine makes a nice aperitif when served with a slice of lemon in the glass.

Wines from Grape Concentrate

There are various brands of grape concentrates on the market but they mainly come from Mediterranean countries. They all make a pleasant wine but you must try the various brands to ascertain the one you particularly like. Each pack has the instructions on the tin but I often find that additional acid and tannin are required.

When evaluating a concentrate, check the degrees baume. The higher the figure, the greater the concentration. Also, look at the colour when water has been added. Some of the reds are not as deep red as might be expected and their colour is degraded to a reddish brown. These should be avoided. The addition of 3 scented red rose petal heads does improve the bouquet. The concentrates can be used as an addition to a recipe in place of raisins or sultanas to add body to a wine; use 1 pint ($\frac{1}{2}$ litre), instead of 1 lb of raisins or sultanas.

Of all the grape concentrates used as the main base for a wine, I prefer the Muscatel, but this is purely a personal preference.

Grey Owl in their Unican range have brought a new style of concentrate out on to the market and these make very nice wines. The concentrates are of grape concentrate with the addition of fruit bases. They are at present obtainable with the following fruits: apricot, peach, bilberry, cherry, blackberry, etc.

Liqueurs and Damson Gin

Liqueurs

For those not wanting to delve too deeply into the subject, liqueurs can be very easily made at home successfully but I am afraid not cheaply. However by using one of your own highly alcoholic sweet wines you can make them more cheaply than you can buy them and you can make a small quantity of a great variety of liqueurs. The process is simple. You make a highly alcoholic syrup as a base and then add the particular liqueur flavour you desire. Here are the materials you require:

One bottle alcoholically strong sweet wine which is not too strong in flavour.

One bottle Polish Spirit 140% proof.

Sugar syrup made by boiling 1 lb sugar (454 gms) in $\frac{1}{2}$ pint ($\frac{1}{2}$ litre) of water and allowing it to go cold.

To obtain a base of a strength of 45% proof: mix 6 fl ozs (168 ml) sugar syrup and 19 fl ozs (632 ml) sweet wine with $4\frac{1}{2}$ fl ozs (126 ml) Polish Spirit. Stir well.

To obtain a base of 70% proof spirit: mix 8 fl ozs (126 ml) sugar syrup, 12½ fl ozs sweet wine (638 ml) and 7½ fl ozs (210 ml) Polish Spirit. Mix well.

Having made your base, you can purchase various liqueur flavourings from the home wine suppliers. Here again get the best quality such as Grey Owl or Noirot flavourings. Add only a few drops of flavouring at a time, then stir well and taste. Remember you can always add; you cannot take away. There is no need to make the whole base up into one particular flavour, but divide your base into several equal parts, trying different flavours to each portion. Make a note of how many drops of a particular flavour you need to suit your own palate so that you will know how much to add should you wish to repeat the recipe.

Damson Gin

Damson Gin is a very rewarding drink if more expensive than home-made wines.

1 lb (454 gms) ripe damsons. One bottle of gin or, if you do not like gin, 1 bottle vodka.

1 lb (454 gms) granulated sugar and 1 screw-topped sweet jar.

Method: Pour the gin or vodka into the sweet jar; add the sugar and stir until dissolved. Prick the skins of each damson with a fork and put them into the sweet jar. Screw on top and shake well. Leave for between 2 to 3 months. Strain off and re-bottle the liquid. The damsons which have been preserved in alcohol can be eaten. The bottled drink is full flavoured and sweet, similar to a liqueur.

The same recipe can be repeated substituting any full-flavoured fruit for the damsons. Use gin if you like a gin background to your drink; if not, use vodka.

Part Two
Beermaking

Chapter 9
Introduction to Beermaking

Beer in one form or another is one of the oldest alcoholic drinks known to mankind. Records of a grain drink are recorded in Egypt as long ago as 3,000 BC, no doubt unrecognisable from the beer drinks of today.

In Great Britain beer is really our national drink. The grain grows well in our climate and in the very early days, honey was used instead of sugar. In those days it was called 'ale' and the name Beer does not appear to have been used until the introduction of hops into the brews around the 16th century. The first organised brewing started in the monasteries and colleges and there are records in existence as early as the 11th century. Sad to relate, even at this early time there was a tax on brewing, and from this it has never escaped.

After the monasteries the individual in every village brewed his or her own beer. Naturally some brewed better beer than others. Some did not have the time and so they started buying from the best brewer in the village, and by a process of evolution, breweries started on a commercial scale.

The breweries grew up around the best water supplies, and thus Burton became renowned for bitter beer and London for brown beer or 'porter'. Across the British Isles were thousands of different breweries, all brewing a style of beer that suited local tastes. In almost all commercial bottle beers the gas in the bottle is injected at the time of bottling. The only 2 bottled beers produced in which the gas in the beer is formed by fermentation in the bottle in the same way that the home brewer uses are Red Triangle Bass and White Shield Worthington. These beers need careful handling in the same way as home brews and also careful pouring, and this, I think, is why the publicans are not keen on stocking them. If you shop around you may come across them, especially in the larger hotels. Buy one and you will find the sediment on the bottom of the bottle in the same way as home brews.

Unfortunately, during the last decade the absorption of so many of the small breweries by 3 or 4 big combines has resulted in almost the complete disappearance of the small brewery, brewing to suit local tastes. If this process continues (and it appears almost inevitable that it will) we will soon only have the choice of no more than 3 different makes of beer. This is the point where home brewing will give every person the chance to make beer to suit his or her own individual palate and the wheel will have turned full circle.

In this age of mass production and uni-taste beers, I will be proud if my book can do a little to bring back the quality beers of an individual flavour that were a feature of this country at the start of the 20th century.

Glossary of Terms used in Beermaking

Acetic Acid	A colourless liquid containing vinegar. The beer will have a vinegar aroma due to over-exposure to air. Once acetified it is beyond redemption.
Attenuation	Brewers' term for fermentation.
Calcium Sulphate	Sometimes called plaster of Paris. Found in proportions in some water, such as used in breweries in Burton-on-Trent. Can now be produced artificially.
Carageen Moss	Sold in natural form or tablets. A type of seaweed added during boiling to assist clarification.
Condition	Carbon dioxide gas found in beers and mineral waters. Commercially injected into bottled beers. Produced in home brews by fermentation of priming sugar when in bottle.
Dextrin	Tasteless, colourless, gummy substance—unfermentable. Gives beer body. Can be purchased in powder form (Burton Brew Body).
Glucose	Artificially produced sugar.
Grist	Name given to various grains used in a mashed brew.
Head	The accumulation of bubbles on top of beer when poured into the glass.
Head Retention Powder	An alginate powder added to a beer when clear and before bottling to assist in forming a head on beer.
Invert Sugar	Sugar that has been treated by heating in a weak acid solution. Assists quick start to fermentation. Used by commercial brewers, some are flavoured with caramel.
Lactose	An unfermentable milk sugar, used to sweeten home brews.
Liquor	Brewers' term for water.
Malted Barley	Barley that has been heated in moist atmosphere and then dried. Should be kept very dry—no more than 2% moisture.

Malt Extract	A syrup obtained by concentrating the extract from malted barley.
Mashing	The extracting of sugars from malted barley by steeping in water for a pre-determined time at pre-determined temperatures.
Priming Sugar	Sugar added in small quantities to bottled beer just prior to securing stopper, to produce a gas (condition) due to action of yeast upon this sugar.
Sparging	The washing through of the grains in sieve with water at pre-determined temperature, to wash out sugar still in grains.
Striking Temperature	The temperature of the water when malted barley is added to start a mash.
Wort	Name given to liquid after malt extract water and hops have been boiled and strained. In the case of beers from mashed grains of malted barley, the name given to the liquid after extraction of the mash and sparging.

Chapter 10
Approaches to Beermaking

Beermaking at home is now rapidly approaching winemaking in popularity. In fact, if it continues at the present rate it will soon be overtaking it. There are many ways of making beer, from the very simple to the complex.

Beer Packs
These are do-it-yourself kits which usually contains malt extract in either dried or syrup form, hops, a yeast, and sometimes some crystal malt for flavouring. You purchase the sugar separately from the grocer but it must be taken into account when pricing the finished beer. There are the nationally-produced beer packs, such as Tom Caxton, whose pack also contains a plastic bag for fermentation and finings for clearing the beer after fermentation. Other national packs are produced by Boots Chemists, Geordie Brews, etc. There are also many hundreds of beer packs under as many names. Some of these are made up by the individual home brew suppliers and others are supplied in bulk from a wholesaler who sells them to the supplier and labels them with the supplier's own labels.

Before attempting to evaluate beer packs it must be understood what part each ingredient plays in the overall beer.

Malt Extract (dried or syrup)
This gives to the beer its malty flavour and at the same time contributes malt sugar for the yeast to ferment into alcohol.

Crystal Malt (grains)
This is malted barley that has been baked from between light brown to medium brown in colour. This is used as an additive in small quantities to give added flavour.

Hops
These are grown on vines mainly in Kent, Worcestershire and Herefordshire. The two best known varieties are Goldings used mainly in bitter beers, and Fuggles used in brown beers and stouts. The hops give bitterness to the beer and, of course, the greater the quantity used, the greater the bitterness. Good quality hops should be from light green to golden in colour according to variety. When rubbed between the palms of the hands they should leave a light stickiness and a sharp bitter aroma. Hops that have gone brown have

been over-exposed to the atmosphere and will give poor results.

Some beer packs contain malt extract in syrup form that has been boiled with the hops before concentration. The advantage to this is that you do not fill the kitchen with the smell which comes from boiling hops and malt extract together. Some do find this smell unpleasant, especially the ladies. But to the true beermaker the aroma is delightful.

I have been greatly concerned when reading the instructions upon some beer packs. I feel that in endeavouring to appeal to the mass market with an 'easy-to-make' approach, some manufacturers have glossed over the only part of beer making that could contain an inherent danger. This is the premature bottling of beer—before fermentation has reached a stage where the residual sugar in the beer would not, when continued to a conclusion, produce too much gas in the bottled beer.

The hydrometer

The only safe way to make beer is with the aid of a hydrometer. This enables the beermaker to tell when the fermentation has been properly completed and no sugar remains in the beer. You can then add just enough sugar to make the required amount of gas in the bottle without any danger of the beer spurting out upon opening and spraying the room. Without the use of a hydrometer, the beermaker—particularly the beginner—may have beer which has stopped fermenting prematurely and, being unaware of the fact, he may bottle the beer too soon. There is then a danger of the fermentation starting up after bottling, with the great danger of burst bottles and possible injury.

Intelligent use of the hydrometer to check that the beer has fully completed its fermentation, will obviate all this danger.

Yeasts

The ideal yeast to use for everything except lager is the British top fermenting beer yeast. For lager a bottom fermenting lager yeast—Saccharomyces Carlbergensis—should be used.

Yeast in beer is of greater importance than yeast in winemaking. A baker's yeast will make a beer, but will produce an off-flavour not found when a genuine top fermenting beer yeast is used. It is not possible to tell the difference between the various yeasts in their natural state. A top fermenting beer yeast will stay at the top of the fermenting wort and after 3 days form a thick layer which helps to protect the brew from air infection. The lager yeast forms on the bottom of the container.

The advantage of a beer pack is that it is simple and no knowledge is required to produce an acceptable drink. If you use a beer pack with a hopped wort you do not get the smell of hops boiling. The big disadvantage with beer packs is that you have to accept the amount of flavour and bitterness decided by the persons that make up the packs. It takes away one of the main advantages of home brewing—that is that you can make a beer that suits your own individual palate.

The best way to evaluate a beer pack is *not* to read the maker's claims as to the amount of beer the pack will make. It is sometimes claimed that a pack will produce 5 gallons (23 litres) of beer. This would be achieved by using the minimum amount of malt extract and the maximum amount of sugar which, incidentally, is not covered by the cost of the pack. This type of pack will produce a high alcoholic thin, low-flavoured beer. The ratio of malt extract to finished beer should be between 2 lbs (907 gms) of malt extract per 3 gallons (14 litres approx) of finished beer for the ideal ration, and from 1 lb (454 gms) malt extract per 2 gallons (9½ litres) of finished beer as just about acceptable. Any higher ratio of finished beer to weight of malt extract will give a thin beer.

Ingredients used for Beermaking
Malt Extract
The choice of malt extract is a matter of personal likes. They all have approximately the same amount of Specific Gravity. Edme, Unican, Forest Maltings, Pains and Munton and Fisons—are all producers of top-class malt extract, among the national producers. There are many more upon the market under different names as they are packed with the supplier's own Trade Name on the label. My choice of malt extract is Itona Controlled Analysis, made in Wigan. My preference for Itona is because it is produced with a high Dextrin content. This is what gives beer its body. The point when using Itona C.A. malt extract is that it is not 100% fermentable, and your wort will only ferment or (to use the brewers' term for fermentation) attenuate down to an S.G. of 10. When it reaches this stage there is no residual sugar left in the beer and the 10° registered is the Dextrin which is tasteless, unfermentable and unsweetened. The Dextrin content gives your beer body and also assists in the head retention. As I say, the particular brand you use is a matter of personal choice.

Additional Grains
These are called adjuncts and are grain malts described as Crystal for bitter beers; Chocolate or Black Malt for brown beers and stouts.

Flaked Maize is also used. It is said to give bitter beer a dry finish. I have included it and have not found that it appeared to make any noticeable difference. Oatmeal (flaked) is used when making Oatmeal Stout. The addition in small quantities of some of these adjuncts will give slight differences of flavour to your beer but the best advice is to keep your recipes simple. If you talk to any Head Brewer you will find that they do not use recipes that have every grain possible added. They rely mainly on simple recipes.

Hops

The best hops for bitter beer are Goldings and, for brown beer and stouts, Fuggles. Other varieties are available such as Northern Brewer and Bullion. These have a very high bitterness ratio and should be used very sparingly. If I am making bitter beer I use Goldings or Fuggles and sometimes, for a slightly more bitter effect, I add 3 to 4 hop flowers of Northern Brewer per gallon. With hops—as with all beermaking ingredients—buy the best quality available, even if a little dearer. It will repay you in the long run.

For lager beers a special type of hop is used. This is the continental hop, such as Saar or Hallertau. Unlike the British hop they only have male flowers and so there will not be any seeds. Now we are in the EEC there is strong pressure from the Continent for us to abandon British hops and replace them with the seedless Continental variety. After all these years this would be impracticable, and I am sure British hop merchants will resist this pressure as it could put them out of business.

Sugars

The usual sugar used by home brewers is the granulated white sugar for pale beers and brown or demerara for browns and stouts. The suppliers sell invert sugar which starts the fermentation a little quicker than granulated sugar but it is more expensive: whether the extra cost justifies its use is debatable. If the commercial brewer wants a beer with a sweet finish he stops the fermentation a little early. His filtering system is so good that he can filter all yeast out of the beer and it remains sweet and stable with no fear of refermentation starting up. This is not possible for the home brewer and yet we still like to make brown beers and some stouts with a sweet finish. We achieve this by fermenting to dryness in the usual way and, after clearing and just prior to bottling, we add lactose—an unfermentable sugar. The amount you use is a matter of personal taste. I use 4 ozs (114 gms) per gallon (4½ litres). Take ½ pint water (284 ml) and add

4 ozs lactose, stir and bring to the boil until it clarifies and then add to the beer and stir well. Remember that the beer will still require priming before bottling.

Water

In the brewing trade they never refer to water as such but prefer to call it liquor. This is no doubt due to an ingrained dislike of the term 'watered beer'. The brewing industry of this country was originally built up around the water supply. The bitter beers were centred around Burton-on-Trent, where the water had a high calcium sulphate content. The brown beers were made around the soft water districts, such as London and Dublin. In latter years the natural water supply was not so important, as the chemist can reproduce any style of water. At the present time opinion is divided between Head Brewers as to the value of this long-established practice. Some of the experts now feel that the chemical content of the water is not as important as they used to think. Chemicals are available to the home brewer to add to the water to change its content from hard to soft or *vice-versa*, but unless you know the chemical content of the water before any additions and then add exactly the right amount to balance it, the process is very hit or miss, and unless your water is one of the two extremes it is better to leave well alone.

Yeasts

These have already been dealt with under 'beer packs'. If you can get a beer yeast from a local brewery, by all means do so. The only thing to watch is that the yeast you obtain is a good settling yeast that will remain firm on the bottom of the bottle. With their great filtering systems most breweries go for a fast fermenting yeast, irrespective of its settling qualities. They can do this as they can filter the yeast out of their brews before bottling—something we cannot do. Always make a yeast starter for each brew as this will get your beer off to a good start. Make it in a quart jug as it is much more active than a wine yeast, and if made in a bottle it will rise out of the bottle.

Additives

Beer nutrients are available if the fermentation sticks to assist in getting it going again, but generally they are not needed. There are two important additives that have come on the home brew market in recent years that have greatly improved the quality of home brews.

The first of these is Dextrin in powder form. This is a white powder, completely soluble in beer, and it is tasteless and non-fermentable. When added to the beer prior to bottling and stirred until dissolved it increases the body in your beer and also assists in head retention. This is not needed when using Itona C.A. malt extract as this particular extract has a high Dextrin content.

It should be added to those malt extracts that normally ferment right out, that is to say they finish with a gravity of 1·000. It is sold under various trade names. One that I recommend is called Burton Brew Body.

The second important additive is one that has been on sale to the commercial brewer for many years but has only just become available on the home brew market. This is a heading powder that is far in advance of the old heading liquids of some years ago, guaranteeing a good head retention on all your beer. It is a white powder sold commercially as Manucol Ester B, and is an alginate and quite safe to use. This is now available to home brewers under various names and, here again, I have only seen it described as 'Heading Powder'. The only difficulty is that, firstly, you only need a minute quantity, and it quickly 'jells' in beer if you do not spread it on the surface of the beer like a fine dust.

The quantity you use is about 3–4 grains ($\frac{1}{4}$ gram per gallon). The best way to add the M.E.B. is to take a small bottle approx 4 ozs (114 gms), shake in the required amount of powder and then half fill the bottle with water. Screw on the stopper and shake vigorously until the powder has completely dissolved in the water. It is now ready to add to your beer. This is done after the beer has been fined and is ready for bottling. Priming is still necessary.

After adding the M.E.B. in liquid form, stir the beer well to ensure an even mixture. The result in the head retention after using this additive will be quite startling.

Priming Sugar

This is sugar added to the beer after fermentation has been completed to give the yeast sufficient sugar to make the beer gassy without danger of bursting bottles or beer gushing out of the bottles upon opening. The beer is fermented to dryness, cleared and ready for bottling. Granulated sugar is added to each 1 pint bottle at the rate of a level teaspoonful. The bottle is sealed with a screw stopper, plastic re-seal or a crown cork, according to the style of bottle and then the beer is stored in a warm place until gassy. The only way to tell if the beer is gassy is to open a bottle and see if bubbles rise in the bottle. If they do, immediately re-seal. If one bottle is gassy it is safe to assume that all the other bottles are also gassy. The beer is then removed to a cool place until wanted for drinking. For the best results, leave the bottles in store for about 6 weeks to mature and then the head will be creamy and lasting.

Carageen Moss
Brewers call this a copper finings. That is to say it is added to the beer at the boiling stage. It can be purchased in its natural state or in tablet form. If bought in the tablet form, use as per the instructions. Carageen Moss is a type of seaweed and, if used in its natural state (it is sold to make jellies) only use it at the rate of 4 grains ($\frac{1}{4}$ gm) per gallon 15 minutes before the end of the boil. The addition of Carageen Moss assists in the eventual clearing of the beer, but remember it is an addition to the use of normal beer finings and not in place of them. Do not add more than the amount required.

Chapter 11
Beer from Malt Extract

Equipment

One of the troubles that besets the home winemaker or beermaker is that they are often attracted to the hobby from the point of view of economy. They are told that beer can be made for as little as 4p per pint, and that the absolute minimum of equipment is required. This, basically, is true and I agree that to start with you should only acquire the absolute minimum. The only danger to this practice is that there is a tendency to use one of the household saucepans for boiling, even if it really is not quite big enough. This is all right until you have definitely decided that the results from your beermaking are to your liking and you plan to make it a regular hobby. Once this point is reached you should spend a little money on getting the correct equipment. The cost of beermaking is so low that money spent on this equipment is money well spent. Far too often I have seen home brewers, even after years in the hobby, still making-do with second-rate vessels and giving themselves double the work, when this could be halved with a little expenditure.

The following equipment is required:

Two 5-gallon plastic dustbins.

A number of 2 gallon plastic buckets.

At least five 1 gallon jars with airlocks.

1 large wooden spoon.

1 sieve (beginners can use a metal sieve)

Serious beermakers should buy a wooden-sided confectioners' sieve with as large a diameter as you can afford.

One 3 gallon boiling pan (beginners can make do with a 2 gallon pressure cooker, used minus the top).

As many screw-top lemonade bottles as you need. Try to get those with a plastic screw top rather than those with the metal top.

For those wishing to show in competitions:

1 pint beer bottles with screw tops, or 1 pint beer bottles with tops that will take either plastic re-seals or crown corks.

For those using crown corks:

A crown-corker machine.

6 ft × $\frac{1}{4}$ in (2 metre × $5\frac{1}{2}$ mm) clear plastic tubing with glass U bend.

One hydrometer and jar.

One large funnel and 1 small funnel.

Method for making a brew with Malt Extract

Into a 3 gallon (14 litre) saucepan pour 2 gallons (9½ litres approx) of water. To this add: 2 lbs (907 gms) malt extract and 2 ozs (57 gms) Golding hops. Bring to the boil and continue boiling for 45 minutes. Stir regularly for the first 10 minutes and then occasionally throughout the boil. Strain the contents through your sieve. The beer at this stage is called the wort.

Leave the wort to go cold. The wort will now be clear with a sediment at the bottom of the container. Syphon off and filter the sediment through filter paper (for this, kitchen paper will prove effective as filter paper). Add the filtered wort to the main bulk. Now add cold water and sugar until the quantity is 3 gallons of wort with a gravity of 1·040.

Now stir in contents of yeast starter bottle and stir the wort well. Cover with loose cover and stir as often as possible for 3 days. Each day wipe the inside of the container above the wort level with a damp cloth to clean off yeast that has splashed up when stirring.

If you are using a brewery top fermenting yeast then after 3 days of fermentation you will get a thick deposit of yeast on the surface of the wort. This should be skimmed off and the wort given a vigorous stirring.

Continue fermentation until the gravity is within 4 degrees of the finished gravity. If you are using a malt extract with Dextrin added, such as Itona C.A., the finished gravity will be 1·010; if using a malt extract without Dextrin the finished gravity will be 1·000. As I say, when within 4° of the finishing gravity, skim off yeast and syphon beer into gallon jars. Insert airlocks and corks and ferment out to the finished gravity.

When fermentation has stopped, allow 1 day to settle. Then syphon off sediment, wash out the jars and return the beer. Into each gallon jar add 2 teaspoonsful of beer finings. Replace airlocks and stand jars in cool place for 3 days. After 3 days syphon off the sediment into a 2 gallon bucket. Now add Heading Powder and stir well.

Now half-fill bottles with beer and add 1 teaspoonful (flat) of sugar to each bottle. Then fill up each bottle with beer to within ¾ in. (19 mm) of the bottom of the stopper. Screw stoppers up tight. Store bottles in a warm place until beer is gassy. Then remove to a cool place; the beer is now ready to drink, but will improve with keeping for 6 further weeks.

Note: Any grains that may be in the recipe should be added at the boiling stage. If a sweet brown beer or sweet stout is being made the lactose is added at the same time as the heading powder.

Lager Beer
The same process, using lager malt extract, lager hops (Hallertau or Saar) and a lager yeast.

The system for making any style of malt extract beer is the same —they only vary in the amount of sugar used, according to whether you want a strong beer or not. Various additional grains, such as crystal malt or black malt in brown beers or stouts, are put in at the boiling stage but the system of fermentation and clearing is the same.

Recommended Recipes
All the following beer recipes have been tried, tested and approved. The rate of hops per gallon of beer is a matter of personal taste. If you wish your beer to have more bitterness than that produced by the recipe then increase the hop rate. If you desire less bitterness, decrease the hop rate. The same applies to the amount of malt extract per gallon. For more malty flavour, increase the ratio of malt per gallon; if less maltiness, decrease the amount of malt per gallon. Always use a true beer yeast; top fermenting for British style beers, and bottom fermenting lager yeast for lagers. As with wine, so with beer: variation can be made in the recipes you use but make sure that you do not alter the balance of the recipe. In all malt extract brews the weight ratio of malt extract per gallon should be much greater than the weight of sugar per gallon of beer. Failure to maintain this will produce thin beers.

Bitter Beer (Malt Extract) using Itona C.A.
To make 3 gallons beer (approx 14 litres):
2 lbs (908 gms) Itona C.A. Malt Extract
2½ ozs (71 gms) Golding hops
Beer Yeast starter
Water and sugar to give 3 gallons with starting gravity 45

Method: Take a large saucepan (3 gallon size). Pour into it contents of 2 lb tin of Itona C.A. Malt Extract. Pour some boiling water into the tin and stir to wash out all the malt extract and add to saucepan. Pour in 2 gallons (approx 9½ litres) of cold water and stir until extract has mixed with water. Add hops and bring to boil. Keep stirring for about 10 minutes after boiling point is reached. This will prevent boiling over. Then adjust heat to keep the mixture boiling vigorously, and continue to boil for between 45 minutes and 1 hour. Take a large polythene container (approx 5 gallons or 23 litres). Place 2 runners across top and stand a wooden-sided sieve on the runners. Strain malt and hop water (the Wort) through sieve. Stand in a cool place until wort is cold. Take syphon tube with U bend and syphon clear wort from the sediment. The sedimentary remains can be filtered through a large funnel into the gallon jar, using kitchen paper as filter paper. Wash out container and return the clear wort into it. Add sugar and water to make quantity up to 3 gallons with starting gravity of 45. Stir in contents of the yeast starter jug. Stir as often as possible for first 3 days. Now take a clean damp cloth and wipe inside of container clean above yeast level.

   Note: Itona C.A. Malt Extract will be completely fermented to dryness when the S.G. reaches between 8 and 10. Ferment on until S.G. reads 14, then syphon off sediment into gallon jars and insert airlock. Ferment on until dryness. Leave one more day to settle then syphon off sediment. Wash out gallon jars with cold water and return beer. Now add 2 teaspoonsful of beer finings per gallon; insert airlock and stand in a cold place for 3 days.

   Syphon off clear beer into buckets. Take a 4 oz (112 ml) bottle, add required amount Manucol Ester B heading powder and half fill with water. Screw on stopper and shake until powder has dissolved into water. Now stir this into clear beer. The addition of the heading powder is optional. Now pour beer into screw-top beer bottles, adding 1 flat teaspoonful of sugar to each bottle. Screw stoppers on tight and store in a warm place, for about 10 days. To test if beer is ready, unscrew one stopper. If bubbles rise in bottle, beer is ready and can be moved to a cool place. If bubbles do not rise, leave in a warm place until they do. The beer is now ready for drinking, but will improve if kept in a cool place for between 4 and 6 weeks.

Bitter Beer using Edme Malt Extract
To make 3 gallons:
2 lbs (908 gms) tin Edme D.M.S. malt extract
2½ ozs (71 gms) Golding hops
Water and sugar to give starting gravity 35
4 ozs (114 gms) Burton Brew Body (optional)
Head powder M.E.B. (optional)
Finings
Beer yeast starter

   Method: Pour malt extract into 3 gallon saucepan and pour over 2 gallons cold water. Add hops and bring to boil, stirring regularly. Boil for 1 hour. Strain the wort through a sieve and stand to go cold. When cold, syphon off clear wort. Filter sediment and add clear wort to the rest. Add sugar and water to make 3 gallons with a starting gravity of 35. Stir in yeast starter and ferment on, stirring regularly for

3 days. When fermentation is down to S.G. 6, pour into gallon jar, insert airlock and ferment to dryness S.G. 0. Leave 1 day to settle. Now syphon off sediment, wash out gallon jars and return beer. Add 2 teaspoonsful of beer finings per gallon, insert airlocks and leave in a cold place for 3 days to clear. Now syphon off sediment, add Heading Powder, as described in previous recipe and stir in 4 ozs Burton Body Brew, per gallon. This will raise the S.G. from 0 to about 9. Do not worry if it is unsweetened and non-fermentable. You have just given your beer more body. Now add 1 teaspoonful of sugar per bottle of beer and bottle as for previous recipe.

The two previous recipes (Bitter Beer using Itona Malt Extract, and Bitter Beer using Edme or similar Malt Extract, can be varied by the addition of 2 ozs (57 gms) Crystal malt added at the boiling stage and then proceed as recipe.

Lager using Malt Extract
To make 3 gallons (14 litres):
2 lbs (908 gms) Itona C.A. Malt Extract
1¼ ozs (40 gms) Hallertau hops
Lager yeast starter
Water and sugar to make up to 3 gallons with starting gravity 50
    Method: As for Bitter Beer Itona C.A. recipe.

London Brown Beer using Malt Extract
To make 3 gallons:
½ lb (227 gms) Itona C.A. Malt Extract
2 lb tin Itona Stout Malt Extract
1½ ozs (45 gms) Fuggles hops
12 ozs (341 gms) Lactose
British Beer yeast starter
Water and sugar to give 3 gallons with starting gravity 45
    Method: As for Itona Bitter beer recipe until beer is cleared and then put 4 oz lactose in saucepan with a cup of water. Bring to boil and then stir in cleared beer. Bottle, adding 1 teaspoonful of sugar per bottle.

The above recipe can be varied by the addition of 4 ozs (114 gms) Crystal malt at boiling.

Stout using Malt Extract
To make 3 gallons:
2 lb tin Itona stout malt

2 ozs (57 gms) Crystal malt
3 ozs (85 gms) Patent black malt
1½ ozs (45 gms) Fuggles hops
Water and sugar to make 3 gallons with starting gravity 50.

Method: As for Bitter beer recipe, adding the grains to the saucepan at the start of boiling with hops. Then proceed as per bitter beer recipe.

Milk Stout using Malt Extract
To make 3 gallons:
2 lb tin Itona stout malt
4 ozs Crystal malt grains
2 ozs Patent black malt
12 ozs Lactose
1½ ozs Fuggles hops
Water and sugar to make 3 gallons with starting gravity 50.
British top fermenting beer yeast.

Method: As for London Brown, adding malts at the start of the boil. Add lactose as described when beer has been cleared.

Making Beer from Hopped Worts (Extracts)
There are numerous firms selling malt extract which has been hopped and the extract is in the style of the beer it is designed for—Bitter Beer, Pale Ale, Lager, Irish Stout, Milk Stout, Barley Wine. With these hopped extracts you only have to add water and sugar according to the maker's instructions and, when cold, add yeast and ferment on as per the instructions. In the first place I suggest you make them up according to the instructions, to see which suits your particular palate. If you wish to experiment you can make your own additions or vary the recipe to suit yourself.

The following suggestions are how you can vary these beers:

1. If you wish to make it more bitter, boil the hopped wort with some extra hops.

2. Reduce the amount of beer to be made. If the wort is for 3 gallons, make it up into 2 gallons.

3. If you wish to have more body in your beer from the hopped wort, make the beer according to the maker's instructions, then when it is fermented and cleared, stir in 4 ozs Burton Brew Body per gallon of beer.

Chapter 12
Beer from Grain Malt (The Mashing System)

The making of beer from grain malt is the same system the commercial breweries use to make their beers, although it must be admitted that they can exercise greater control over their beermaking than the home brewer can. It is generally accepted, amongst the leading home brewers, that a beer well made from grain is superior to that made from malt extract, but it is a more complex system and more time-consuming.

Before going into the details of the system it is important to appreciate what happens.

For brewing, special varieties of barley are grown that are most suitable for brewing. When the barley has been threshed it is sacked and left for what is known as a waiting period. This is about 6 weeks. It is not known why this is necessary—suffice it to say that it is. The barley in its natural state would not be suitable for brewing as the grains would be too tough. Because of this the barley has to go through a treatment known as 'malting'. This is done by a Maltster. The grain is moistened and kept in a warm damp atmosphere for about 14 days. The whole procedure is controlled and, as a result, the barley starts to grow small rootlets. During this process the texture of the grain alters. The grain is then kiln dried, the rootlets shrivel and are blown away. The barley has now been turned into malted barley and is ready for the brewer.

Before the brewer can use the malted barley it has to be crushed to the correct texture. Too close a crushing will turn the grain into flour and it will go lumpy when added to water; too coarsely crushed and the water will not be able to react on the starch in the barley grain. From this it will be obvious that the home brewer cannot hope to buy malted barley whole and then crush it to the correct degree. Always buy your malted barley grains already crushed. The grains must not be allowed to be in a damp atmosphere. They should always be kept in sealed polythene bags and kept biscuit dry. When the crushed grain is brought in contact with hot water, the water extracts certain sugars at different temperatures and this is why, temperature control in this system, which is called mashing, is of such great importance. When the temperature is kept at 140°F (60°C) the sugars extracted are 99% fermentable. When the temperature is 152°F (66°C) the extraction will be approx 75% maltose and 25% Dextrins. The Dextrins are unfermentable. By varying the temperature you can vary the style of extract.

In the commercial brewery the mashing period in total is about 4 hours. The home brewer needs only to mash for between 1 hour and $1\frac{1}{2}$. The commercial brewer dealing in large quantities of grain has to be more economical than the home brewer.

The liquid from the mashing is called the Wort and once it has been strained from the grain it has to be boiled. The boiling takes place in the presence of the hops and has to be a very vigorous boil——called by the brewers a 'thumping' boil, and the duration should be for 2 hours. The Wort is then strained from the hops and cooled as quickly as possible. The commercial brewers use what is called a Paraflow. The Wort is forced through thin tubes surrounded by jackets through which is passed cold water. This causes rapid cooling. The Wort is then ready to receive the yeast. We cannot emulate the controls exercised by the brewers but with a little care we can come close enough to get the desired results.

Equipment Required

A certain amount of extra equipment is required to make beer by the mashing method, including a long immersion thermometer about 12 in (305 mm) in length. The mashing can be done in a saucepan but it is much more time-saving to make a quantity of between 5 gallons (23 litres) and 10 gallons ($45\frac{1}{2}$ litres approx). The best vessel in which to do the mashing is a large boiler, either gas or electricity. I use a Burco boiler which is heated by electricity, and the larger size is ideal. You can pick them up secondhand quite cheaply.

Bitter Beer

To mash the grain you need a much larger saucepan or boiling container than you would require when using malt extract because the malted barley grains take up more space in the container. The crushed malted barley grains are used at the rate of 2 lbs (908 gms) per gallon ($4\frac{1}{2}$ litres) of beer.

1. Pour $\frac{2}{3}$ of the total of finished beer to be made, in the form of water, into your heating container, e.g. if the recipe is to make 3 gallons ($13\frac{3}{4}$ litres approx) you would pour 2 gallons ($9\frac{1}{4}$ litres approx) of water into the heating container.

2. You then heat this water until it reaches 165°F (74°C). This is called the striking temperature.

3. You now sprinkle the crushed malted barley over the surface

of the water, stirring the whole time until all the grain has been mixed in and is well integrated with the water. Check the temperature of the mash and adjust by heating or cooling until it levels off at 152°F (66°C). Make sure that the heating is switched off.

4. Place lid on heating container and cover with any old blanket to insulate it. Keep all doors of the room closed to avoid draughts that might cool the container.

5. Twice in the first half-hour of the mash, stir the mash well and check the temperature. It should remain at 152°F (66°C) but if it drops, switch on the heat for a few moments until the temperature reaches 152°F.

6. Keeping the container insulated, leave the mash to stand for the next half hour.

7. The mash has now been progressing for a total of 1 hour.

8. Place your 5 gallon plastic container (23 litres) close to your mash container. Place 2 flat wooden runners across the top of the plastic container and stand your wooden-sided sieve upon the runners. At the same time, heat a quantity of water to 165°F (74°C).

9. Take a Pyrex jug and fill the sieve with the mash; replace the lid on the heating container. Now fill the Pyrex jug with water at 165°F (74°C) and wash it over the grains in the sieve.

10. When the Wort—as the liquid is called at this stage—has drained through, empty the grains from the sieve and refill with grains from heating container and again wash through with water at 165°F. Use 1 pint ($\frac{1}{2}$ litre) of the water to each sieve full of grains.

11. Repeat the process until all the mash has been strained through the sieve and then wash out the heating container.

12. Return strained Wort to the heating container and add hops.

13. Switch on heat and boil the Wort vigorously for about 2 hours, adding Carageen Moss at the rate of 4 grains ($\frac{1}{4}$ gm) per gallon if using natural moss, or as per instructions if in tablet form.

14. Replace sieve on top of polythene container and strain the Wort through sieve.

15. Place polythene container of Wort outside to cool.

16. When Wort is cold, carry container as carefully as possible to avoid undue disturbance of liquid, and put it on to table.

17. The Wort should be clear, apart from the bottom inch (25 mm). Using a syphon transfer the clear Wort to another plastic container, leaving the sediment in the bottom of the original container.

18. The sediment can now be filtered through a funnel lined with kitchen paper and the resultant clear Wort is added to the main bulk.

19. Now add cold water and sugar to bring the bulk up to the required amount of beer to be made, at the starting gravity required, at the same time making sure that the sugar has been dissolved by stirring.

20. Place container of Wort in a room with a temperature of about 65°F (18°C) and stir in contents of the yeast starter bottle.

21. Stir regularly during the first 3 days.

22. Skim off surface yeast, cleaning inside of container above the yeast level with a damp cloth. Stir well.

23. Continue fermentation until the Specific Gravity drops to within 4° of dryness. Then transfer beer into gallon jars and insert airlocks and corks.

24. Ferment on to dryness.

25. Syphon beer off sediment and return to clean gallon jars. Add 2 teaspoonsful of beer finings per gallon jar.

26. Leave for 3 days to clear.

27. Syphon clear beer into 1 large container. Add Heading Powder as described and stir well.

28. Bottle in screw top bottle, adding 1 level teaspoonful of sugar per bottle.

29. Store in a warm place until gassy.

30. For best results, when gassy, store in cool place for between 4 to 6 weeks.

Remember that, apart from good technique, the most important factor in producing good beer is to buy the best quality ingredients.

Brown Beers and Stouts
The process for these styles of beers is the same as for Bitter Beers just described. The only difference is that the mashing temperature is between 146°F (63°C) and 148°F (64°C) instead of 152°F (66°C).

For sweet beers and stouts, add lactose at the rate of 4 ozs (114 gms) per gallon of beer at the bottling stage.

Lager
Lager originated in Denmark and comes from the German word *Lageren*, meaning storage. The most important advance was the discovery of the lager yeast—*Lenevisiae Carlberggensis*—a bottom fermenting yeast. The Danes ferment their Lager at low temperatures over a long period. They also use a different method of mashing called the Decoction System. There are many variations and the one I shall describe is one of the more straightforward.

Different varieties of malted grains are used and these are available to the home brewer. Special lager hops, such as Hallertau or Saar are used. Less hops per gallon of these hops are used than would be the case with British hops.

Making Lager by Decoction Mashing System
Take your heating container and into it place the lager malted barley grains called for by the recipe. Stir in sufficient cold water to make a fairly stiff mash. Keep stirring, raising the temperature to 122°F (50°C). Hold the mash at 120°F for 20 minutes. Now extract from your heating container $\frac{1}{3}$ of the total mash. The withdrawn mash is heated in another container until it boils. Once boiling, maintain the boil for 20 minutes. Now return the boiling mash to the main heating container, stirring well. This should now bring the heat of the main mash to 150°F (69°C). Maintain this temperature for 1 hour. Then again extract $\frac{1}{3}$ of the total mash and again boil for 20 minutes. Now return the boiling mash to the main mash again. This should bring the main mash to about 170°F (82°C). Let it stand for 30 minutes.

Place the wooden-sided sieve on runners across the top of the plastic bin. Fill the sieve with the mash and sparge with water at 170°F (82°C). Sparge the remainder of the mash this way until the quantity of Wort is within 3 pints ($13\frac{3}{4}$ litres approx) of the total amount of beer to be made. Now add your lager hops and boil the Wort vigorously for 2 hours, adding Carageen Moss for the last 15 minutes of the boil.

Strain the Wort through the sieve and stand in a cool place until it is cold. Syphon off the clear Wort, leaving behind the sediment. Now add sugar and cold water to make the quantity up to the required amount at the required Specific Gravity. Now stir in the contents of the lager beer yeast starter bottle. Ferment out in the usual way and proceed as for Bitter Beer from this point on.

It will be appreciated that making lager by the decoction mashing is a tedious business, but if well done, makes a true lager. The above is just one of the many decoction systems. There are other but they are even more involved and only the dedicated home brewer will attempt them.

Recommended Recipes
The system for making beers from the following recipes has been given, step by step, earlier in this chapter.
Bitter Beer (Burton Style)
To make 3 gallons:

6 lbs (2¾ kgs approx) crushed malted barley grains
3 ozs (85 gms) Golding hops
Carageen Moss
Sugar and water to make up to 3 gallons with starting gravity 45
Top fermenting beer yeast starter

Bitter Beer (Strong)
To make 2 gallons (9½ litres approx):
3¼ lbs (1½ kgs) crushed malted barley grains
4 ozs (114 gms) crushed Crystal malt
1 oz (29 gms) Golding hops
¼ oz (8 gms) Northern Brewer hops
Sugar and water to make up to 2 gallons with starting gravity 50
Carageen Moss
Top fermenting beer yeast starter

London Brown
To make 2 gallons:
3¼ lbs (1½ kgs) crushed malted barley grains
6 ozs (171 gms) crushed Crystal malt
3 ozs (85 gms) crushed Black malt
12 ozs (341 gms) Malt extract (Dried medium dark)
1 oz (29 gms) Fuggle hops
8 ozs (227 gms) Lactose
Water and sugar to give 2 gallons with starting gravity 45
Carageen Moss
Top fermenting beer yeast starter

Milk Stout
To make 2 gallons:
3¼ lbs (1½ kgs) Crushed malted barley grains
8 ozs (227 gms) Crystal malt crushed
8 ozs (227 gms) Demerara sugar
4 ozs (114 gms) Black malt crushed
1 oz (29 gms) Fuggle hops
Carageen Moss
8 ozs Lactose
Water and any additional sugar to give 2 gallons with starting
    gravity 46
Top fermenting beer yeast

Barley Wine
To make 2 gallons:
4½ lbs (2 kgs approx) crushed pale barley grains
1 lb (454 gms) Malt extract
8 ozs (27 gms) crushed Crystal malt
8 ozs Demerara sugar
2½ ozs Golding hops
Carageen Moss
Water and sugar to give 2 gallons with starting gravity 70
General purpose yeast.
This is one beer that needs a wine yeast and not a beer yeast. It may
take 3 to 4 weeks to ferment out in the gallon jars. Bottle in nip bottles.
This is a very strong brew and should be drunk with care.

Irish Stout
To make 2 gallons:
3¾ lbs (1½ kgs) crushed malted barley grains
8 ozs (227 gms) crushed black malt grains
4 ozs (114 gms) crushed Crystal malt grains
4 ozs crushed roasted barley
8 ozs dried malt extract medium dark
1 oz (29 gms) Fuggles hops
¼ oz (8 gms) Northern Brewer hops
Top fermenting beer yeast starter
Water and sugar to make 2 gallons with starting gravity 50

Lager
To make 2 gallons:
3¾ lbs (1½ kgs) crushed Lager malted barley grains
12 ozs (341 gms) dried Pale malt extract
1 oz Hallertau hops
Carageen Moss
Water and sugar to make up to 2 gallons with starting gravity 50–55
Bottom fermenting Lager yeast starter

Low Alcohol and Beer-style drinks (Shandies)
Grey Owl produce a hopped wort with full instructions to make a
lemonade shandy and a ginger beer shandy. Both make a delightful
low alcoholic drink, suitable for those who want to drink in quantity
without the fear of consuming too much alcohol. They are packed
under their Unican trade mark and make a pleasant change.

Draught Beer

Draught beer is made to the same system as bottled beer up to the point where the beer is cleared. Now add 1 oz (40 gms) of sugar per gallon (4½ litres) of cleared beer and stir until dissolved. The beer is now poured into a pressure keg and sealed. The best pressure kegs are fitted with an injector for injecting CO_2 gas into the container. The beer is left for about 7 days to become gassy. It must be remembered that the gas injector should only be used after some of the beer has been drawn off to drink. The injector is not for making the beer gassy but it is to produce pressure to force the beer out of the barrel when the level of beer, due to consumption, has dropped, and without the use of the gas would be difficult to pour from the tap.

Some home brewers have managed to obtain secondhand the professional dispensers used in small clubs. These are used in conjunction with large carbon dioxide cylinders but professional advice should be sought before they are used.

Chapter 13
Faults and Their Cure

1. Many problems can be solved before they appear by making sure that all equipment is well washed and dried after use and sterilised before re-use.

2. When fermenting your beer, make sure that your container is away from any draughts.

3. Always use a pure beer yeast (except for barley wine).

4. A yeast may be re-used after having been taken from the yeast crop from your previous brew. However it must be stored in your fridge and should only be used once. A fresh crop should then be taken from the brew it was used to ferment.

5. Yeast 'bite'. This causes an acrid bitterness to the brew. This can be caused by the ring of sediment around the top inside of the container just above the yeast level being left in contact with the beer. Avoid this by wiping clean with a damp cloth.

6. If possible, buy your crushed malted barley grains in bulk and keep in polythene bags well sealed to avoid dampness penetrating. Keep hops in airtight bags in a cool place.

7. Lack of head retention. Use M.E.B. head retention powder, as per supplier's instructions and this fault can be eliminated.

8. Always pour beer into dry glasses.

9. After washing glasses always rinse well in clear water, avoid use of detergents.

10. Lack of condition. That lack of gas in the bottle. This is caused either by too little priming sugar, leaky stoppers or storing the beer in too cool a place immediately after priming. Always make sure the rubber stoppers on bottles are clean and in good condition.

11. If Crown corks are used instead of screw stoppers, buy a Crown capper machine. They cost a couple of pounds but are well worth the cost.

12. Avoid any undue exposure of your fermenting beer to air. If the beer becomes acetified (vinegar smell), there is no cure and it should be thrown away.

13. When fermenting on in gallon jars, fill the jars to within 1 in. (3 cm) of airlock. Failure to do this may cause a powdery film to form on top of the beer. This is flowers of wine and will ruin your beer.

14. Do not ferment at above 68°F (20°C).

15. Always use a hydrometer to check fermentation.

16. Always ensure that fermentation has ceased before adding priming sugar.

17. Beers are better after maturing for between 4 to 6 weeks.

18. Always buy the best quality ingredients.

19. Avoid sticking fermentations by keeping your beer well stirred during fermentation.

Chapter 14
Making Beer for Competition

Read the schedule carefully. Most of the larger shows follow the standards laid down by the National Guild of Beer Judges.

Use 1 pint beer bottles in green, brown or colourless glass. The stoppers should be either Crown corks, plastic re-seals or screw tops (the screw stop going into the top of the bottle and not around the top).

The bottle should be filled to within $\frac{1}{2}$ in (13 mm) and $\frac{3}{4}$ in (19 mm) from the bottom of the stopper.

Always use new Crown corks or new plastic re-seals or, if screw stoppers, use new rubber rings.

It is not possible to make a brew for a special competition and be sure of success. Depending upon how frequently you make a brew of beer, the best way is to bottle 3 bottles of beer up to show standard with every brew. Mark the date and style of beer upon every bottle you fill.

When you come to drink the first bottle from a new brew, evaluate it, and if it is of good quality, place 3 show bottles on one side. If you do this, when a competition comes up you will probably have at least 6 groups of 3 bottles from your previous brews. Now take 1 bottle from each group. Pour out a glass of beer from each, evaluate it for clarity, colour, condition, head retention, bouquet and taste. Decide which group of 3 bottles is the best and then put one of the unopened bottles from this group in the next show. If you follow this system it will ensure that your best beer is in the show.

If you win a show it will not always follow that a further bottle from the same group will win at the next show. Remember it will depend upon the quality of the opposition.

A good show beer should have a hard sediment on the bottom of the bottle that will remain fast even when the bottle is opened. This is dependent on the yeast and a good settling yeast is hard to find. There is a way to overcome this and that is to rebottle your beer prior to showing. Firstly, you place 3 bottles of your beer in the fridge for a week before re-bottling. This is to quieten down the CO_2 gas. After 7 days, take the 3 bottles from the fridge and clean the outsides with a damp cloth. Now take your empty show beer bottle and wash it carefully inside and out, but do not use detergent. Now take 2 large clean bowls. Stand your empty beer bottle in one of the bowls. Place a small funnel (one with an air-vent if possible) in the bottle. Now open your first bottle of beer and pour two-thirds of the contents into the funnel. Keep pouring even though the beer will gush out of the funnel down the sides of the bottle into the bowl. Then place the bottle in the other bowl and pour the beer that has escaped into the first bowl into the funnel.

Open the second bottle and repeat the process until the beer in your show bottle is filled to the correct level, using part of the contents of the third bottle of beer if necessary. As soon as your bottle is filled to the correct level—seal. In this way you should ensure 1 bottle of beer without sediment but with sufficient condition (bubbles) to satisfy the judges. The only snag to this system is that you cannot tell whether you have sufficient condition in your bottle until it is opened by the judge. If you have to send your beer a long distance to the show, then the above system is well worth trying.

Index

INDEX OF BEER RECIPES

GENERAL INDEX